THE OPEN UNIVERSE

THE OPEN UNIVERSE

An Argument for Indeterminism

KARL R. POPPER

From the POSTSCRIPT TO THE LOGIC OF
SCIENTIFIC DISCOVERY
Edited by W. W. Bartley, III

London

First published 1982

Paperback edition 1988

Reprinted 1991
by Routledge
11 Fetter Lane, London EC4P 4EE

Printed in Great Britain at the University Press, Cambridge

British Library Cataloguing in Publication Data available

ISBN 0 415 07865 2

TO ERNST GOMBRICH

CONTENTS

Note on Numbering of Sections. The sections in each of the three volumes of the *Postscript* are numbered consecutively, beginning with section 1. The original section numbers, indicating the order of the sections within the *Postscript* as a whole, are given in starred brackets in the Tables of Contents. Ed.

CONTENTS

CONTENTS

EDITOR'S FOREWORD

THIS book, *The Open Universe: An Argument for Indeterminism,* is the second volume, and contains the centerpiece of the argument, of Sir Karl Popper's long-awaited *Postscript* to *The Logic of Scientific Discovery.* Although it was written in the mid-fifties, it has never before been published. Yet it contains the most sustained and important treatment of the problems of determinism and indeterminism of which I know.

The *Postscript* to *The Logic of Scientific Discovery* was written mainly during the years 1951–56, at the time when *Logik der Forschung,* Popper's first published book (1934), was being translated into English as *The Logic of Scientific Discovery.*

The different volumes of the *Postscript* were originally part of a series of Appendices to *The Logic of Scientific Discovery,* in which Popper proposed to correct, expand, and develop the ideas of his first book. Some of these Appendices were in fact included in *The Logic of Scientific Discovery* when it was published in 1959. But one group of the Appendices took on a life of its own, and gradually grew into a single, closely-integrated work—far exceeding the original *Logik der Forschung* in length. It was decided to publish this new work—called the *Postscript: After Twenty Years*—as a sequel or companion volume to *The Logic of Scientific Discovery.* And it was accordingly set in type, in galley proofs, in 1956-57.

Within a few months of the anticipated publication, however, the project came grinding to a halt. In *Unended Quest,* his intellectual autobiography, Sir Karl has reported of these galley proofs: 'Proof reading turned into a nightmare. . . . I then had to have operations on both eyes. After this I could not start

xi

proofreading again for some time, and as a result the *Postscript* is still unpublished.'

I remember this time vividly: I went to Vienna to visit Popper in the hospital there shortly after his operation for several detachments of both retinas; and we worked on the *Postscript* as he was recuperating. For a long time he could barely see, and we were very much afraid that he would become blind.

When he was able to see again, a great deal of work was done on the *Postscript*: several sections were added, and thousands of corrections were made to the galleys. But the pressure of other work had now become too great, and virtually nothing was added to the text after 1962. During the next, highly productive decade, after publishing *Conjectures and Refutations* (1963), Popper completed and published three new books: *Objective Knowledge: An Evolutionary Approach* (1972), *Unended Quest* (1974 and 1976), and (with Sir John Eccles) *The Self and Its Brain* (1977), as well as many papers. These were the years, and the works, in which his now-famous theory of objective mind (and of Worlds 1, 2, and 3) was developed, and in which his approach was extended into the biological sciences.

Meanwhile, the *Postscript,* which represented the culmination of Sir Karl's work in the philosophy of physics, went unpublished. But not unread: most of Popper's closest students and colleagues have studied this work, and several have had copies of the galley proofs over the years. It is a source of great satisfaction to those like myself, who have known this book and been deeply influenced by it, to see it finally completed and shared with the general public.

The text that has now been edited for publication is essentially that which existed in 1962. Except in a few places, as marked, no major alterations have been made. It was felt that this was the appropriate approach to a work that had now acquired, through its influence on Popper's students and colleagues, an historical character—some twenty-five years having passed since its composition, and forty-five years since the writing of the original *Logik der Forschung*. Obviously, many points would have been put differently today. But a complete revision by the author would have delayed publication indefinitely.

The editing has included bringing together the different versions of some parts of the text, as they had accumulated over the years; copy-editing the book; and adding bibliographical and other notes for the reader's assistance. A few new additions made by Popper himself are clearly marked: they are presented in brackets and marked with a star: *. My own brief editorial and bibliographical notes are also in brackets, followed by the abbreviation 'Ed.'. Here I have in general followed the practice established by Troels Eggers Hansen, the editor of Popper's *Die beiden Grundprobleme der Erkenntnistheorie* (written in 1930–32 and published in 1979). Popper has been able to check the editorial work at a series of meetings which we have held at various places over the past two years—in Heidelberg, Guelph, Toronto, Washington, D.C., Schloss Kronberg, and at his home in Buckinghamshire. He has also added new prefaces to all of the volumes and a new afterword to the second volume.

One major alteration in presentation has been made, at my own suggestion. To publish this large work under one cover would have been possible, but would have meant a heavy and unwieldy book beyond the means of many students of philosophy. Parts of the *Postscript*—including *The Open Universe: An Argument for Indeterminism*—will be of wide interest, of concern not only to philosophers and students of philosophy but also to a wider public.

These parts are also, on the whole, independent of one another. This led me to suggest that the work be published in three separate volumes, in matching format, the whole constituting the *Postscript*. After some hesitation, Sir Karl agreed with this proposal, and also with the titles which I suggested for the three volumes.

Thus the *Postscript* is being published as follows:

Realism and the Aim of Science   (Volume I)
The Open Universe: An Argument for Indeterminism   (Volume II)
Quantum Theory and the Schism in Physics   (Volume III).

Although these three volumes of the *Postscript* can easily be read separately, the reader should be aware that they build a connected argument. Each volume of the *Postscript* attacks one or another of the subjectivist or idealist approaches to knowledge; each constructs one or more components of an objective, realist approach to knowledge.

Thus in the volume now called *Realism and the Aim of Science* Popper pursues 'Inductivism', which he sees as the chief source of subjectivism and idealism, through four stages: logical, methodological, epistemological, and metaphysical. He develops his theory of falsifiability, and charts its effects in demarcating scientific, non-scientific, and pseudo-scientific views from one another. And he presents his theory of corroboration as a way to express rational preference for one theory over another without resorting either to the subjective 'certainties' or to the objective 'justification' of conventional philosophies. In that first volume Popper also discusses his relationship to those historical figures in philosophy, such as Berkeley, Hume, Kant, Mach, and Russell, who have contributed importantly to the subjectivist tradition; and he gives detailed replies to contemporary philosophical and scientific critics. Popper also attacks the subjective interpretation of the probability calculus, an interpretation that is rooted in the belief that probability measures a subjective state of insufficient knowledge. In *The Logic of Scientific Discovery*, Popper had championed an objective interpretation of the probability calculus, using for this purpose the frequency interpretation. Now he also criticizes the frequency interpretation. In its place he presents in detail his own propensity interpretation—an interpretation which has, during the past twenty years, found many champions. These ideas and arguments are applied and developed in the remaining volumes.

In *The Open Universe: An Argument for Indeterminism*, Popper presents a critique of both 'scientific' and metaphysical forms of determinism, and argues that classical physics does not presuppose or imply determinism any more than quantum physics does. Yet he finds that metaphysical determinism continues to underlie the work of many contemporary quantum theorists, opponents of determinism included. Popper traces the continuing role played within physics by subjective interpretations of probability to these metaphysical deterministic presuppositions.

There is a deep connection between the arguments of the first and second volumes, in their mutual concern with the freedom, creativity, and rationality of man.

The first volume, in its consideration of justification and rationality, rebuts a subjectivist and sceptical claim about the limits of criticism—and therewith the limits of rationality. If such a limit existed, then serious argument would be futile; and the appearance of it would be illusory.

The second volume, in its treatment of determinism, champions the claim that our rationality is limited in respect to the prediction of the future growth of human knowledge. If such a limit did *not* exist, then serious argument would be futile; and the appearance of it would be illusory.

Popper thus argues that human reason is unlimited with regard to criticism yet limited with regard to its powers of prediction; and shows that both the lack of limitation and the limitation are, in their respective places, necessary for human rationality to exist at all.

In Volume III, *Quantum Theory and the Schism in Physics*, Popper reviews and rebuts an array of arguments and 'paradoxes' that are widely used to defend an idealist outlook. Conjecturing that the problems of interpretation of quantum mechanics can be traced to problems of the interpretation of the calculus of probability, Popper develops his own propensity interpretation of probability further. And then he gives a sweeping critique of some of the leading interpretations of quantum theory, attempting to resolve their well-known paradoxes and to exorcise 'the Observer' from quantum physics.

His concluding 'Metaphysical Epilogue' weaves together the themes of the entire *Postscript*, in an historical and programmatic study of the role of metaphysical research programmes or interpretations in the history of physics.

The Editor wishes to express his gratitude to The American Council of Learned Societies and to the American Philosophical

Society for their generous support of his editorial work on these volumes; and to Professors Donald T. Campbell and F. A. von Hayek for their advice and support. He also wishes to thank his secretary, Nancy Artis Sadoyama, for her devoted and unfailing assistance.

ACKNOWLEDGEMENTS

I wish to take this opportunity to thank my colleague John W. N. Watkins for the great encouragement which his unflagging interest has been to me. He has read this volume in manuscript and in proof, and has made the most helpful suggestions for improvements. It was at his suggestion that I decided to publish this *Postscript* as a separate work rather than, as originally planned, as a series of Appendices to *The Logic of Scientific Discovery*. But even more important for the completion of the work than these suggestions was his interest in its ideas.

I also wish to thank the co-translators of *The Logic of Scientific Discovery*, Dr Julius Freed and Lan Freed, who read most of this volume in galley proof, and made a great number of suggestions for improving its style. [They both died many years before its publication. Ed.]

Joseph Agassi was, during the period that this book was written, first my research student and later my research assistant. I discussed almost every section with him in detail, very often with the result that, on his advice, I expanded a statement or two into a whole new section—or, in one case, into a whole new part. [It became Part 2 of *Realism and the Aim of Science*.] His co-operation was of the greatest value for me.

I also wish to thank the London School of Economics and Political Science, which made it possible for me to benefit from Dr Agassi's assistance, and the Center for Advanced Study in the Behavioral Sciences (Ford Foundation) in Stanford, California, for giving me the opportunity of working uninterruptedly from October 1956 to July 1957 on the galley proofs of this book, and for making it possible for Dr Agassi to help me during this period.

PENN, BUCKINGHAMSHIRE, *1959*.

ACKNOWLEDGEMENTS

Professor W. W. Bartley, III, was my student, and later my colleague at the London School of Economics, from 1958–63, and he worked closely with me during 1960–62 on this book. In 1978 he kindly consented to act as Editor of the *Postscript*. I am grateful to him for his assistance and for undertaking this arduous task. I am indebted to him more than I can say.

It is also a pleasure to thank several other persons who have in the intervening years worked with me on this *Postscript*, in particular, Alan E. Musgrave, David Miller, Arne F. Petersen, Tom Settle, and Jeremy Shearmur. Of these, David Miller and Arne Petersen should be specially mentioned because of the immense amount of work which they both did at various periods before 1970.

The London School has continued through all these years to help me by appointing a research assistant. For the thirteen years since my retirement in 1969 it has done so with the help of a grant from the Nuffield Foundation, to whom I wish to express my thanks. Chiefly responsible for this arrangement were my friend and successor, Professor John Watkins; the late Sir Walter Adams, Director of the School; and the present Director, Professor Ralf Dahrendorf, to whose warm friendship and great interest in my work I am deeply indebted.

Had the *Postscript* been published in the 1950s, I should have dedicated it to Bertrand Russell: Professor Bartley has told me that a letter to this effect exists in the Russell Archives at McMaster University.

I may mention, finally, that this *Postscript* (together with the translation of *The Logic of Scientific Discovery*) seemed to me almost ready in 1954. It was then that I chose its original title, 'Postscript: After Twenty Years', with an allusion to the publication of *Logik der Forschung* in 1934.

PENN, BUCKINGHAMSHIRE, *1982*.

PREFACE 1982

As Professor Bartley explains in his Foreword, this volume was written before 1956, as part of my *Postscript* to the *Logic of Scientific Discovery*. It was not intended to discuss human freedom and human free will, even though these were really the problems that stood behind it.

There were various reasons why I did not wish to discuss such matters explicitly at the time I wrote this book. The main reason is that the *Postscript* was intended, like *The Logic of Scientific Discovery*, to which it is a sequel, to discuss the physical sciences, their methods and some of their implications, physical cosmology, and the role of the theory of knowledge in the physical sciences.

A second reason is that I felt that several of the problems gathered around the problem of human freedom were somewhat muddled by what philosophers have written about them. This muddle begins at least with Hume, one of the very greatest philosophers of all time. It is, I think, connected with the fact that common sense is muddled about these problems. For (1) common sense inclines, on the one hand, to assert that *every* event is caused by some preceding events, so that every event can be explained or predicted if we know all the relevant preceding events in sufficient detail. On the other hand, (2) common sense attributes to mature and sane human persons, at least in many situations, the ability to choose freely between alternative possibilities of acting; and hence responsibility for such action.

Now (1) and (2) seem to clash, and the problem is whether this clash is real or only apparent. Hume and many determinists have tried, with ingenuity and subtlety (in my opinion with too much subtlety) to show that (1) and (2) do not really clash, so that one can be a determinist and, at the same time, speak of the freedom of action. The arguments on which this position is based are, however, largely verbal. They depend upon the verbal analysis of the meaning of such words as 'free', 'will', and 'action'; and upon the analysis of such questions as, 'Could I have done otherwise than I did?' These verbal analyses are quite futile and have led modern philosophy into a morass. But there is another approach.

My own departure, and my own approach to these questions, I take not from Hume (who has dominated the British discussion of these matters), but from Laplace. In his *Essai philosophique sur les probabilités*, 1819, published some fifty years after Hume's *Treatise*, Laplace wrote:

> We ought . . . to regard the present state of the universe as the effect of its anterior state and as the cause of the one which is to follow. Assume . . . an intelligence which could know all the forces by which nature is animated, and the states at an instant of all the objects that compose it; . . . for [this intelligence], nothing could be uncertain; and the future, as the past, would be present to its eyes.[1]

This position, which is (as I explain in the body of this book) much stronger than common sense, I call 'scientific' determinism. It is a position with which most physicists, though not all (I am thinking for example of Charles Sanders Peirce), would have agreed at least prior to 1927. This Laplacean determinism asserts that the state of the universe at any moment of time, future or past, is completely determined if its state, its situation, is given at some moment, for example, the present moment. I regard such Laplacean determinism—confirmed as it may seem to be by the *prima facie* deterministic theories of physics, and by their marvellous success—as the most solid and serious difficulty in the way of an account of, and a defence of, human freedom, creativity, and responsibility. Certainly Laplace's strong clear statement of determinism, which goes beyond common sense and which also is deeply intertwined with the history of western science, is far superior to the loose formulation given above as (1).

[1] Translated as *A Philosophical Essay on Probabilities*, 1951, pp. 4–5.

Laplacean determinism can, however, be opposed—and I do oppose it in this book. For my own part, I am no determinist. And I have taken as my task in this book to make room within physical theory, and within cosmology, for indeterminism. Thus I argue that Laplacean determinism is not tenable, and that it is, moreover, required neither by 'classical' nor by contemporary physics. This is a serious task, having nothing to do with fundamentally verbal quibbles.[2] My own discussion will then be on a cosmological plane: I shall discuss the character of our world rather than the meaning of words.

But in order to avoid misunderstandings I wish to make it quite clear that whenever in this book I speak of 'scientific' determinism (with quotation marks before and after 'scientific'), I have in mind an *allegedly* 'scientific' doctrine, an *allegedly* 'scientific' determinism. It is a doctrine which owes its popularity, and its influence even among great scientists, to its apparently scientific character, to the fact that it is widely believed to be part of science, especially Newton's and Einstein's theories of gravitation and Maxwell's theory of the electromagnetic field.

In the course of my argument, I shall be able to develop in opposition to determinism a position which also tries to transcend (2) above.

In any case, I want to state clearly here something that is apparent both in *The Open Society and Its Enemies* and in *The Poverty of Historicism*: that I am deeply interested in the philosophical defence of human freedom, of human creativity, and of what is traditionally called free will—even though I believe that such questions as 'What is freedom?' or 'What does "free" mean?', and 'What is will?', and similar questions, and the attempt to clarify them, may lead into the morass of language philosophy. This book is then a kind of prolegomenon to the question of human freedom and creativity, and makes room for it

---

[2] I may remind my readers that the avoidance of verbal issues has been one of my main guiding lines from the very start of my career. See the Preface to the First Edition, 1934, of *The Logic of Scientific Discovery*, particularly the quotations from Schlick and Kant. See also *The Open Society and Its Enemies*, 1945, Chapter 11, and *Unended Quest*, 1976, section 7.

physically and cosmologically in a way that does not depend on verbal analyses.

With respect to the commencement of the first chapter of the book, a word may be said about my views on intuition.

I regard intuition and imagination as immensely important: we need them to invent a theory. But intuition, just because it may persuade and convince us of the truth of what we have intuited, may badly mislead us: it is an invaluable helper, but also a dangerous helper, for it tends to make us uncritical. We must always meet it with respect, with gratitude, and with an effort to be severely critical of it.

CHAPTER I

KINDS OF DETERMINISM

I INTEND to set forth here my reasons for being an indeterminist. [1] I shall not include among these reasons the intuitive idea of free will: as a rational argument in favour of indeterminism it is useless. A man may well believe that he is acting deliberately, and of his own free choice, when in fact he is acting under the influence of suggestion, or of compulsion, or of drugs. But once we have succeeded in rejecting the idea of determinism by arguments which do not involve an appeal to our intuitions regarding free will, it may perhaps be possible, to a limited extent, to re-establish the validity of these intuitions; for the counter-examples just mentioned might then be treated as special cases—as cases of delusion, perhaps, by which these intuitions are temporarily made unreliable. However, none of these questions will be discussed here. What I am going to do in the following is to criticize the commonsense arguments, the philosophical arguments, and especially the scientific arguments, which have been used in support of determinism.

My central problem is to examine the validity of the arguments in favour of what I call *'scientific'* determinism; that is to say, the doctrine that the structure of the world is such that *any event can*

[1] This part of the *Postscript* may be considered as an improved version of my paper, 'Indeterminism in Quantum Physics and in Classical Physics', *British Journal for the Philosophy of Science* 1, No. 2, pp. 117–133, and No. 3, pp. 173–195. [On this issue see also Popper's *Of Clouds and Clocks: An Approach to the Problem of Rationality and the Freedom of Man* (St. Louis, 1966), reprinted in *Objective Knowledge* (London, 1972), pp. 206–55. Ed.]

be rationally predicted, with any desired degree of precision, if we are given a sufficiently precise description of past events, together with all the laws of nature.

The problem is relevant mainly because exponents of the quantum theory often present the situation in the following way. Classical physics, they say, entails what I call 'scientific' determinism; and only quantum theory forces us to reject classical physics, and 'scientific' determinism with it. In opposition to this view, I intend to show that even the validity of classical physics would not impose upon us any deterministic doctrine about the world.

In criticizing determinism, I shall be concerned with a view of the physical and biological sciences which was held by physicists, practically without exception, until 1927, and by Einstein, it seems, almost until his death in 1955.[2] It was held also by

[2] [In fact, by 1954 Einstein appears to have changed his mind fundamentally with regard to determinism. Thus a letter from Wolfgang Pauli to Max Born, dated 31 March 1954, has now been published, wherein Pauli reports of conversations with Einstein at Princeton: 'In particular, Einstein does not consider the concept of "determinism" to be as fundamental as it is frequently held to be (as he told me emphatically many times) . . . In the same way, he *disputes* that he uses as criterion for the admissibility of a theory the question: "Is it rigorously deterministic?" Einstein's point of departure is "realistic" rather than "deterministic", which means that his philosophical prejudice is a different one.' See *The Born-Einstein Letters* (New York, 1971), p. 221, or *Albert Einstein–Hedwig und Max Born: Briefwechsel: 1916–1955* (Munich, 1969), p. 293.

Popper had visited Einstein in Princeton in 1950, and had at that time delivered as a lecture (which Einstein attended) the essay on 'Indeterminism in Quantum Physics and in Classical Physics' (*British Journal for the Philosophy of Science* 1, pp. 117–133, and pp. 173–195) that was eventually to be the basis for this volume of the *Postscript*. In his intellectual autobiography, Popper writes of his three conversations with Einstein at this time: 'The main topic of our conversation was indeterminism. I tried to persuade him to give up his determinism, which amounted to the view that the world was a four-dimensional Parmenidean block universe in which change was a human illusion, or very nearly so. (He agreed that this had been his view, and while discussing it I called him "Parmenides".) I argued that if men, or other organisms, could experience change and genuine succession in time, then this was real. It could not be explained away by a theory of the successive rising into our consciousness of time slices which in some sense coexist; for this kind of "rising into consciousness" would have precisely the same character as that succession of

philosophers such as Spinoza, Hobbes, Hume, Kant, Schopen-hauer, J. S. Mill, and (at least until 1927) by M. Schlick. Schlick was still in two minds about the problem in 1930, as the following interesting quotation shows.

> Since this assumption that *all* events are subject to universal laws is usually described as the principle of universal causation, I may put [my thesis] in this way: Every science presupposes the principle of universal causation . . . All experience supports the belief that this presupposition is satisfied, at least as far as it is necessary for all purposes of practical living, in all contacts with other men and with

changes which the theory tries to explain away. I also brought in the somewhat obvious biological arguments: that the evolution of life, and the way organisms behave, especially higher animals, cannot really be understood on the basis of any theory which interprets time as if it were something like another (aniso-tropic) space coordinate. After all, we do *not* experience space coordinates. And this is because they are simply nonexistent: we must beware of hypostatizing them; they are constructions which are almost wholly arbitrary. Why should we then experience the time coordinate—to be sure, the one appropriate to our inertial system—not only as real but also as absolute, that is, as unalterable and independent of anything we can do (except changing our state of motion)?

'The *reality of time and change* seemed to me the crux of realism. (I still so regard it, and it has been so regarded by some idealistic opponents of realism, such as Schrödinger and Gödel.)

'When I visited Einstein, Schilpp's *Einstein* volume in *The Library of Living Philosophers* had just been published; this volume contained a now famous contribution of Gödel's which employed, against the reality of time and change, arguments from Einstein's two relativity theories. Einstein had come out in that volume strongly in favour of realism. And he clearly disagreed with Gödel's idealism: he suggested in his reply that Gödel's solutions of the cosmological equations might have "to be excluded on physical grounds".

'Now I tried to present to Einstein-Parmenides as strongly as I could my conviction that a clear stand must be made against any idealistic view of time. And I also tried to show that, though the idealistic view was compatible with both determinism and indeterminism, a clear stand should be made in favour of an "open" universe—one in which the future was in no sense contained in the past or the present, even though they do impose severe restrictions on it. I argued that we should not be swayed by our theories to give up common sense too easily. Einstein clearly did not want to give up realism (for which the strongest arguments were based on common sense), though I think that he was ready to admit, as I was, that we might be forced one day to give it up if very powerful arguments (of Gödel's type, say) were to be brought against it.'

See K. R. Popper: *Unended Quest*, 1976, p. 129–30, or P. A. Schilpp, ed.: *The Philosophy of Karl Popper*, 1974, Vol. I, p. 102. See also section 26 below. Ed.]

nature, and also for even the utmost precision which technology requires. But whether the principle of causality is valid absolutely and everywhere, without even the slightest exception—that is to say, whether determinism is correct—that we do not know. What we know, however, is this: that it is impossible to decide the issue between determinism and indeterminism by mere thinking and speculating, by weighing the number of arguments *pro* and *con* (all of which would be pseudo-arguments anyway). Such an enterprise is bound to create a ridiculous impression, especially if one thinks of the overwhelming armoury of experimental and logical craftsmanship with which contemporary physics is now cautiously closing in to attack the problem whether or not the principle of causality is valid even for the hyperfine events within the atoms.[3]

I have quoted this passage because it is, in many ways, representative of the view which I intend to criticize: that the principle of causality is the same as the thesis of determinism, and that we know from experience that it is correct at least for all practical purposes: for '*all* events', although perhaps not for 'absolutely' all events, 'everywhere, without even the slightest exception'—a doubt raised by quantum theory. Also, because I intend to take up the challenge inherent in Schlick's suggestion that the problem is arguable, but only with empirical arguments, while speculative thinking on these matters can only use 'pseudo-arguments', bound to create a 'ridiculous impression'. Indeed, I do not feel that it is entirely beyond speculative thought to improve a little upon the empirical arguments.

[3] M. Schlick, *Fragen der Ethik*, 1930, p. 106 (the translation is mine, the italics are Schlick's. *Cp.* also Schlick's essay in *Naturwissenschaften* 8, 1920, esp. p. 467). It is a little surprising to find that the determinist philosophy, and with it our problem, are now being dismissed—incidentally, by a recent defender of Schlick's—as an '*eighteenth century* bogey' (*Mind*, 1954, p. 331). Time marches on, no doubt, and, no doubt, time will, in time, solve all our problems. Yet strangely enough, even we old fogies who remember the times and problems of Einstein or Schlick have to make quite an effort to recall the fact that these men produced their bogies even before Laplace produced his (calling it 'an intelligence') in the *Essay* of 1819.

1. *Determinism: Religious, 'Scientific', and Metaphysical.*

The intuitive idea of determinism may be summed up by saying that the world is like a motion-picture film: the picture or still which is just being projected is *the present*. Those parts of the film which have already been shown constitute *the past*. And those which have not yet been shown constitute *the future*.

In the film, the future co-exists with the past; and the future is fixed, in exactly the same sense as the past. Though the spectator may not know the future, every future event, without exception, might in principle be known with certainty, exactly like the past, since it exists in the same sense in which the past exists. In fact, the future will be known to the producer of the film—to the Creator of the world.

The idea of determinism is of religious origin, although there are great religions which believe in indeterminism—the doctrine that at least *some* events are not fixed in advance. (Since St. Augustine, at least, Christian theology has for the most part taught the doctrine of indeterminism; the great exceptions are Luther and Calvin.) Religious determinism is connected with the ideas of divine omnipotence—complete power to determine the future—and of divine omniscience, which implies that the future is known to God now, and therefore knowable in advance, and fixed in advance.[1]

Besides religious determinism, there is a form of the doctrine of determinism which I shall call *'scientific'*.

Historically, one can look upon the idea of a 'scientific' determinism as the result of replacing the idea of God by the idea of nature, and the idea of divine law by that of natural law.

---

[1] The doctrine of divine omnipotence leads to difficulties, however. Some of these are internal or logical. (Does omnipotence include the power to change the past, or does it mean only power over the future?) It clashes to some extent with the doctrine of determinism (especially if it introduces a fundamental distinction between past and future). It also clashes to some extent with the doctrine of divine omniscience. (For if everything is known to God, then the future is known; it is therefore fixed in advance, and unalterable, even by God Himself.) I shall not discuss here the ethical difficulties involved in the doctrine of divine omnipotence, such as the ethical problem of whether it is not evil to teach the adulation of power.

5

Nature, or perhaps the 'law of nature', is omnipotent as well as omniscient. It fixes everything in advance. By contrast with God, who is inscrutable, and who may be known only by revelation, the laws of nature may be discovered by human reason, aided by human experience. And if we know the laws of nature, we can predict the future from present data by purely rational methods.

It is characteristic of all forms of the determinist doctrine that *every* event in the world is predetermined: if at least one (future) event is not predetermined, determinism is to be rejected, and *indeterminism* is true. In terms of what I call *'scientific'* determinism, this means that if at least one future event in the world could not in principle be predicted by way of calculation from natural laws and data concerning the present or the past state of the world, then 'scientific' determinism would have to be rejected.

Thus the fundamental idea underlying 'scientific' determinism is that the structure of the world is such that every future event can in principle be rationally calculated in advance, if only we know the laws of nature, and the present or past state of the world. But if *every* event is to be *predictable, it must be predictable with any desired degree of precision*: for even the most minute difference in measurement may be claimed to distinguish between *different* events.

Although the idea of 'scientific' determinism seems, historically speaking, to be a kind of translation of religious determinism into naturalistic and rationalistic terms, it is of course possible to see the idea of 'scientific' determinism in a different light. One can present it, for example, as resulting from a somewhat sophisticated criticism of the commonsense view of the world according to which one can divide all events into two types: the predictable events, such as the changes of the seasons, or the diurnal and annual motions of the sun and of the fixed stars, or the working of a *clock*; and the unpredictable events, such as the vagaries of the weather, or the behaviour of *clouds*. [2]

[2] [See K. R. Popper: 'Of Clouds and Clocks,' *op. cit.* When Popper read this footnote and reread this page, he noted that he had forgotten that he had first mentioned the image of clouds and clocks in this section of the *Postscript*, and so

Now this commonsense view of the difference between *clocks* and *clouds* may be criticized by raising the somewhat sophisticated question of whether these two types of events are *really* different or whether only the unsatisfactory state of our knowledge makes them appear to be different; *whether the behaviour of clouds would be as predictable as that of clocks if only we knew as much about clouds as we know about clocks.*

This question, or rather, this conjecture, turned into a conviction as soon as an advance in scientific knowledge made it possible to predict the movements of planets or 'vagabonds'—once the notorious symbols of caprice—as precisely as those of the fixed stars themselves. It was this success, the success of Kepler's laws and of Newton's dynamics of the heavens, that led to the almost universal acceptance of 'scientific' determinism in modern times.

The power of the belief in 'scientific' determinism may be gauged by the fact that Kant, who for moral reasons rejected determinism, nevertheless felt compelled to accept it as an undeniable fact, established by science. This led to an antinomy in his philosophical system which he could never resolve to his own satisfaction. As I shall try to show, however, Newtonian mechanics does not entail 'scientific' determinism. If I am right in this, then Kant was mistaken in believing that by accepting Newtonian mechanics he had committed himself to accepting 'scientific' determinism; and his unresolved antinomy simply does not arise.

The critical discussion of 'scientific' determinism will be our main task. But besides religious and 'scientific' determinism, a third version of the deterministic doctrine will also have to be discussed, if only briefly. It may be described as *metaphysical determinism*. [3]

The metaphysical doctrine of determinism simply asserts that

did not use this section when writing 'Of Clouds and Clocks'. Thus there may be some discrepancies between the two presentations. Ed.]

[3] [*(Added 1981) I avoided, or tried to avoid, the term 'ontology' in this book, and also in my other books; especially because of the fuss made by some philosophers over 'ontology'. Perhaps it would have been better to explain this term, and then to use it, rather than to avoid it. However that may be, questions of terminology are never important.]

all events in this world are fixed, or unalterable, or predetermined. It does not assert that they are known to anybody, or
predictable by scientific means. But it asserts that the future is as
little changeable as is the past. Everybody knows what we mean
when we say that the past cannot be changed. It is in precisely the
same sense that the future cannot be changed, according to
metaphysical determinism.

Metaphysical determinism is clearly not testable. For even if
the world constantly surprised us, and showed no sign of any
predetermination or even of any regularity, the future might still
be predetermined, and even foreknown by those able to read the
book of destiny. Metaphysical indeterminism is also untestable.
For even if the world had a completely regular and deterministic
appearance, this would not establish that no undetermined event
of any kind exists. Now lack of testability, or of empirical
content, is indicative of logical weakness (not meaninglessness, of
course): a doctrine may be logically too weak to be tested. And
for the same reason, it may be entailed by some other doctrine.
Thus metaphysical determinism is, because of its weakness,
entailed by both religious and 'scientific' determinism; and it may
be described as containing only what is common to the various
deterministic theories. It is irrefutable just because of its weakness. But this does not mean that arguments in its favour or
against it are impossible. The strongest arguments in its favour are
those which support 'scientific' determinism. If they collapse,
little is left to support metaphysical determinism. For this reason,
I am going to examine them first. Only towards the end of my
discussion (in section 26), will I advance some more direct
arguments against the acceptance of metaphysical determinism.

In the following sections, commonsense arguments and
philosophical arguments in favour of 'scientific' determinism will
be examined first; only afterwards will I turn to the arguments
based upon classical physics.

2. *Why-Questions. Causality and 'Scientific' Determinism.*
In the preceding section I suggested a commonsense or *prima
facie* distinction between predictable and non-predictable events,

or between *clocks* and *clouds*, and that 'scientific' determinism can be viewed as arising out of a sophisticated criticism of this distinction. Another way for common sense to approach the idea of determinism is through the popular idea of causality. One of the simplest and most plausible arguments in favour of determinism is this: we can *always* ask, of *every* event, why it happened; and to every such why-question we can always obtain, in principle, a reply which enlightens us. Thus every event is 'caused'; and this seems to mean that it must be determined, in advance, by the events which constitute its cause.

We could admit the truth of these considerations without, however, admitting that they can lead us all the way to the idea of 'scientific' determinism. It is, in fact, of considerable interest to pin-point the place where the commonsense arguments end and sophistication begins.

Let us first consider some typical why-questions, and some typical answers to them which are perfectly satisfactory on the commonsense level.

'Why do bees store honey?' Answer: 'Because they need it for food during the winter.' (This is hardly a theoretical statement at all.) 'Why is there a lunar eclipse today?' Answer: 'Because the earth is standing today between the sun and the moon, so that its shadow falls on the moon.' (This is not yet a statement of theory from which we could predict the eclipse.) 'Why did he die?' Answer: 'Because when he went to a funeral last week, he stood in the rain for nearly half an hour. So he caught a cold which developed into pneumonia; and after all, he was seventy-three.' (Many have survived the ordeal even at seventy-four.)

We may assume that all these answers are perfectly acceptable, and that they give precisely the kind of information asked for. Even children who insatiably reiterate their why-questions are not usually asking to be given a 'better' explanation—in the sense of one which would allow them to *predict* events of the kind in question. What they want to be given is, as a rule, merely a statement of further causes—causes which temporally precede those given, or which would motivate them further: they do not reiterate their questions because they want a fuller set of conditions, but because they want to be given a consecutive 'causal chain' of events.

The fact that we can always ask why-questions, and that we can always obtain relevant answers to them has not in itself, then, very much to do with determinism, whether 'scientific' or otherwise.

But we may now go one step farther, and demand that the answers to our why-questions—that is to say, the explanations offered—should indeed consist of initial conditions (causes) from which the facts to be explained can be logically deduced, if the relevant universal laws are given.[1] This is certainly a step away from the popular theory of causation, and towards a more sophisticated theory. Let us accept this demand, and assume, in addition, a 'law of universal causation', to the effect that *every* 'event' can in principle be causally explained in the sense of our demand; that is to say, we assume that there are always 'causes' (initial conditions) and universal laws which would allow us to deduce the 'event' in question. This is a strong assumption. But it does not quite amount to 'scientific' determinism yet, and this for several reasons.

First, the commonsense idea of an 'event' (which is to be causally explained) is mainly qualitative. So the demand of 'scientific' determinism that we should be able to predict the event *with any desired degree of precision* certainly goes beyond the commonsense idea of universal causation. It may be common sense to ask for a causal explanation of John's feverish condition; but it goes beyond common sense to ask either for an explanation as to why his temperature is between 102.4 and 102.5 rather than 102 or 103, or for a prediction made with the corresponding degree of precision.

Secondly, the common-sense idea of a cause is likewise mainly qualitative. The realization that causes—that is, the initial conditions—are never given to us with absolute precision; that we must therefore be content with initial conditions which are imprecise, to some extent; and that this fact raises its peculiar

[1] *Cp.* section 12 of *The Logic of Scientific Discovery*.

problems: all this goes beyond the commonsense or intuitive idea of causality.

Thirdly, there is the following problem which arises from the two preceding ones: 'scientific' determinism requires the ability to predict every event with any desired degree of precision, provided we are given *sufficiently* precise initial conditions. But what does 'sufficiently' mean here? Clearly, we have to explain 'sufficiently' in such a way that we deprive ourselves of the right to plead—every time we fail in our predictions—that we were given initial conditions which were not sufficiently precise.

In other words, *our theory will have to account* for the imprecision of the prediction: given the degree of precision which we require of the prediction, it will have to enable us to calculate the degree of precision in the initial conditions that would suffice to give us a prediction of the required degree of precision. I call this demand the 'principle of accountability'. It will have to be incorporated into the definition of 'scientific' determinism.

Since the three points mentioned here—and especially the third—clearly do go beyond the popular or commonsense idea of causality, it is conceivable that the popular intuitive idea of causality—even in the strong form of the principle of universal causation—is valid, as far as it goes, while at the same time the doctrine of 'scientific' determinism is invalid.

Thus we must beware of the mistake made by so many distinguished philosophers who have believed that one can validly argue in favour of determinism by pointing out that every event has a cause.

3. *The Principle of Accountability.*

The result of a calculation will not, as a rule, be more precise than the least precise of its data; and a prediction, accordingly, will not, as a rule, be more precise than any of the given initial conditions upon which it is based.[1] If therefore we demand that it

---

[1] This rule holds for most cases but is not universally valid: it does not necessarily apply, for example, to mechanisms capable of *discrete states* only,

shall always be possible to make our predictions as precise as we desire, this demand will not, as a rule, be satisfiable unless we can increase the precision of the relevant initial conditions as much as we desire: the initial conditions will have to be *sufficiently precise* for a solution of the problem set by the prediction task.

For the purpose of defining 'scientific' determinism, a demand to the effect that we must be able to obtain predictions with any stipulated degree of precision provided we are given *'sufficiently precise'* initial conditions would, clearly, be too vague. Such a demand would make our definition trivial. We could always claim that it is satisfied, even if we always fail to derive successful predictions; we could always explain all our failures away by claiming that our initial conditions were not 'sufficiently precise'. To remedy this situation, we have to demand that we must be able to find out, *before* we test the result of our predictions, whether or not the initial conditions are sufficiently precise; in other words, we must be able to determine in advance, from the prediction task (which must state, among other things, the degree of precision required of the prediction), in conjunction with the theory, how precise the initial conditions or 'data' have to be in order to enable us to carry out this particular prediction task. To put it more fully, we must be able to *account in advance* for any failure to predict an event with the desired degree of precision, by pointing out that our initial conditions are not precise enough, and by stating how precise they would have to be for the particular prediction task in hand. Thus any satisfactory definition of 'scientific' determinism will have to be based upon the principle (i.e., the principle of accountability) that *we can calculate from our prediction task (in conjunction with our theories, of course) the requisite degree of precision of the initial conditions.* [2]

---

such as a harmonium, or a typewriter: our information about the *precise* position of the organist's finger on a certain key, for example, may be quite irrelevant for the predicted effect. Word language, especially if written or printed, is essentially of this character, and so are digital computers.

[2] A similar principle was formulated by Pierre Duhem, but in a different context (not in a discussion of determinism) and with a different aim in mind. He

Some prediction tasks are 'accountable'—that is to say, they satisfy the principle of accountability—while other prediction tasks may not be accountable. We may also say of a theory that it is 'accountable' when prediction tasks within it are, as a rule, accountable.

For certain purposes, it may be useful to operate with a somewhat stronger principle of accountability, arrived at by referring to *the precision of the results of possible measurements from which the initial conditions can be calculated,* rather than to the *precision of the initial conditions.* Thus in this stronger sense, a prediction task may not be accountable because we cannot determine from it (and the theory) the requisite degree of precision of possible *measurements* upon which we may base our predictions. Yet it is conceivable that the same prediction task could be accountable in the weaker sense of allowing us to calculate the degree of precision with which the *initial conditions* would have to be given in order to solve it.

This stronger idea of accountability is clearly the more 'realistic' of the two: a theory which is accountable in the weak sense but non-accountable in the strong sense would be one whose determinist character could in principle not be tested by us: it could not be used to support 'scientific' determinism. In other words, 'scientific' determinism requires accountability in the stronger sense. Nevertheless, in what follows I shall always have in mind accountability in its weaker sense, unless I specially allude to the difference between the two senses. The reason is that if a theory is *non*-accountable in the weaker sense (of 'accountable') then it is clearly *non*-accountable in the stronger sense also; in other words, *non*-accountability in the weaker sense of the word 'accountable' entails (or is logically stronger than) *non*-accountability in the stronger sense of the word 'accountable'.

Since 'scientific' determinism entails the principle of accountability, any example of a definitely non-accountable prediction

puts it as follows: 'It is necessary that we shall be able to determine the . . . error that may be allowed to the data if we wish to obtain a result within a definite degree of approximation.' Cp. *The Aim and Structure of Physical Theory,* 1954, p. 143, the third paragraph from the end of chapter iii.

problem, applicable to our own world, would at once destroy the doctrine of 'scientific' determinism. But even if we cannot produce an indubitable example of this kind, it should be clear that *we have no reason to believe in 'scientific' determinism if we have no reason to believe that the principle of accountability is universally satisfied.*

In the next sections I shall try to show that, in at least two fields, some convincing commonsense arguments as well as some famous philosophical arguments in favour of determinism break down just because we have no reason whatever to believe that the principle of accountability is satisfied in those fields.

Our discussion will establish the following. It is possible that we may continue to learn more and more about a certain field; that we may predict more and more events; and that we may continue to increase the precision of our predictions. And yet, this continual growth of our predictive powers may not constitute any valid reason for the belief that 'scientific' determinism is valid within the field. Our predictions may constantly improve and yet, at the same time, be arrived at by methods which do not even suggest that the principle of accountability is satisfied.

Later (in section 17) the problem of the accountability of classical physics will be raised, and it will be shown that there are hardly any reasons to believe that it is accountable in the weaker sense, and very good reasons to believe that it is not accountable in the stronger sense.

4. *The Study of Behaviour and the Principle of Accountability.*

Let us now examine a simple yet very strong argument in favour of determinism.

Indeterminists have sometimes asserted that men, and perhaps to a lesser degree the higher animals, behave very differently from planetary systems or mechanical clocks, and that determinism (even if valid in the field of mechanics) may therefore be invalid in the biological field. Against these views, some determinists have argued as follows.

It is undeniable that we can often predict the behaviour of animals, and also of men, very successfully. Moreover, these predictions tend to become better and better as we learn more and more about the man or the animal; and they may be still further improved by a systematic study of their behaviour. There is no reason why this process of learning more and more about behaviour should ever come to an end. Thus the result of our study of organisms may be expected to be the same as the result of our study of planetary systems. We can express this by saying that the higher organisms belong to the *clock* category. (It does not matter if we find that they are like mechanical clocks, or more like some electronic self-regulating mechanism.) Whether or not the *clouds* also belong to this category may at this point be left open.

This argument—'*the argument from the study of behaviour*', as it may be called—is good common sense, and in my opinion very telling. But it does not achieve its aims; not even if we grant, as I am ready to do, that there is no limit to the possible improvement of our predictions of animal and human behaviour through its closer and closer study. As an attempt to support determinism, the argument from the study of behaviour is simply invalid.

To show this, we need only refer to the principle of accountability. 'Scientific' determinism does not merely assert that we may improve our predictions by increased knowledge, but it demands that *we shall be able to calculate, from our specified prediction task, the degree of precision of our initial information that is needed to carry out the prediction task.*

Now the argument from the study of behaviour contains nothing to suggest that the improvement of our knowledge will help us to satisfy this principle. I happen to be fairly successful in predicting what my cat will do next: whether he will jump on to my desk, and settle down on my writing pad, or whether he will jump on the window sill and from there into the garden; and I am continually learning more about his behaviour. But the behaviour I am learning about consists, in the main, either of (a) significant (or 'goal-directed') actions, or (b) tricks of habit, or ways of doing things. Studying the latter may help to fill in some details in

15

the broad schemata of the former. Nevertheless, when I predict that he will settle on my writing pad, there are many details which I cannot predict. For example, *I may easily be wrong by several inches.*

There is nothing in my learning situation which suggests how these details may be added to the picture. Of course, we may always say that a better knowledge of the relevant initial conditions would reduce the inches as much as we like. *But we simply do not know what kind of initial conditions may be relevant to the prediction task of reducing these inches.* It is not only that we have no theory of behaviour which satisfies the principle of accountability: up to now we have not even an idea of where to look for such a theory.

It will be objected that a precise study of the nervous system, especially the brain, would do much towards closing the gaps in our predictions. This may be quite true, for all I know, and for argument's sake, I will take it for granted here. But it means *giving up the argument from the study of behaviour.* It replaces the commonsense argument that we can learn more and more from studying the behaviour of animals by a completely different argument: by the argument that physiology and physics are deterministic systems.

5. *Critical Temperatures and the All-or-Nothing Principle.*

The fact is that we know so little about these matters that we have not the slightest idea of how to apply our very considerable knowledge of brain physiology to a prediction task such as the one concerning my cat's *precise* position.

But let us assume that we do know how to apply our knowledge about brain physiology. Let us assume, more especially, that what we need are initial conditions which will allow us to predict the contraction of a certain muscle; and in the last instance, initial conditions which will allow us to predict whether or not a certain ganglion (or group of ganglia) will 'fire'.

Now the process of a firing nerve is in many respects analogous to an explosion: the nerve fires suddenly, when a certain electric

16

potential (the end-plate potential) has risen to a certain critical height. If this height is not reached, the nerve does not fire at all. [1] (This is known as the all-or-nothing principle of nervous transmission.) In a similar way, a chemical explosion will take place if a certain critical temperature is reached; and it may be that, below this, nothing happens. [2]

There are, however, grave doubts whether the principle of accountability is applicable to the critical temperature of an explosion; and for precisely analogous reasons, whether it is applicable to nervous transmission. Admittedly, if the temperature is below the critical one, rising slowly but steadily, we can safely predict the time of the explosion. However, accountability entails the thesis that we are able to predict the time of the explosion with as much accuracy as we like. And this thesis, in its turn, involves another: that we are able to make measurements of the temperature, and of its rate of increase, as accurately as we like. But temperature is a mass-effect; it is a molar or a macroscopic quantity. It is essentially an average; and quantities like this cannot in principle be measured as precisely as we wish.

There is every reason to believe that the precise value of the potential at which a given nerve fires is also dependent upon certain other mass-effects. For example, it depends on a fatigue-effect (which, most likely, depends in its turn upon the presence or absence of a sufficient *concentration*—that is to say, a *sufficiently large number*—of molecules of a certain kind). Even if we assume the truth of metaphysical determinism, there is nothing in our present theories to indicate that we shall ever be able to calculate, in general, the necessary precision of the initial conditions from the specifications of the prediction task.

To sum up these considerations, we may say that the brain (whether or not it amplifies elementary quantum processes) is in all likelihood highly sensitive to mass-effects such as tempera-

[1] See, for example, J.C. Eccles, *The Neurophysiological Basis of Mind*, 1953. [See also K. R. Popper and J. C. Eccles: *The Self and Its Brain*, 1977, pp. 541 and 565. Ed.]

[2] See, for example, K.F. Bonhoeffer, 'Modèles Physico-Chemiques de l'Excitation Nerveuse', *Journal de Chimie Physique* 51, pp. 521–9.

tures or the concentration of certain chemicals. (This is far from surprising, considering that our muscular movements are mass-effects, and that they are partially dependent upon other mass-effects such as 'volleys' of nerve-impulses.) But we have no clue, no indication whatever, which allows us to say that the principle of accountability may be applied to these mass-effects; or if so, how it could be applied.

We see how far we have moved from the commonsense 'argument from behaviour', and that indeed nothing in our ordinary experience of learning more and more about behaviour suggests accountability.

Quite generally we may say that even though our knowledge, and with it our power to predict, may steadily increase in a certain field, this fact can never in itself be used as an argument in favour of the view that something like 'scientific' determinism holds for this field. For our knowledge may steadily increase without approaching that very special kind of knowledge which satisfies the principle of accountability.

6. *Clocks and Clouds.*

Since I have had to refer to mass-effects, this is perhaps a good place to criticize the deterministic argument from clocks and clouds, mentioned in section 1 above. I am alluding to the argument that the commonsense distinction between predictable events (the movement of planets, or of clocks) and unpredictable events (the weather, or the movement of clouds) is invalid, and that this distinction will disappear when we obtain as much *knowledge* about clouds—about their laws as well as about their detailed initial conditions—as we have about clocks.

As the example of the planets shows, something is to be said for this argument. Improved detailed knowledge of clouds may indeed go a long way towards assimilating them to events of the clock category. But this assimilation cannot be completely successful, because mass-effects are involved.

Moreover, we can also view the matter the other way round: if we wish to predict the working of clocks in greater and greater detail, we shall have to investigate, for example, the flow of heat in the clock (in order to find out, say, how the length of the pendulum is affected). But this more detailed study would clearly lead to assimilating the clock to a cloud of molecules, subject to movements of a kind which present the same prediction problems as those of a cloud. Thus the convincing argument that with the increase of our knowledge the category of clouds will approximate more and more closely to that of clocks can be countered by pointing out that the opposite also holds.

It is often said that two clocks which are exactly alike will show the same time, and will continue to do so. This may be so, but it is of little interest because we never have two clocks which are exactly alike. Moreover, two clocks or watches serially produced in a factory and looking otherwise perfectly alike will not, in general, continue to show the same time. This is why they are built so that they can be adjusted with the help of a regulating mechanism. After an adjustment has been made, they may keep the same time quite well; but they will not in general look alike any longer: a mechanically important part—the regulating mechanism—may now exhibit a clearly observable difference. This difference had to be introduced in order to make the two clocks more alike in another respect—in keeping time. This shows that superficial likeness may be highly deceptive.

If a clock loses time, a good watchmaker may find the cause—perhaps a speck of dust in the works. The example is interesting because, although it is in keeping with the law of universal causation, it clearly does not satisfy the principle of accountability. No watchmaker could predict, from inspecting the speck of dust, that it would cause a loss of three minutes a day rather than five minutes a day. Nor could he predict that, once this particular speck of dust were removed, the clock would keep time without further adjustment.

7. *Arguments for Determinism from Psychology.*
The arguments from behaviour and from physiology are invalid, as we have seen. The reason is not so much that there is

any difficulty in measuring, say, behavioural initial conditions; it is, rather, that the precision of our behavioural predictions cannot be improved indefinitely by improving the precision of the measurements of the behavioural initial conditions.

But the argument from behaviour is only a version of an older argument, *the argument from psychology*.

Some great philosophers have used this argument to counter the idea of free will, and thereby, indirectly, to support the idea of determinism. This argument goes back a long way. Since the renaissance, it has been perhaps most clearly stated by Hobbes, Spinoza, Hume, and Priestley.[1] As Hobbes puts it, 'the will is also necessarily *caused* by other things whereof it disposes not'; and so 'it follows that voluntary actions have all of them necessary causes'.

Hume introduced the idea of *'inference from motives* to voluntary actions', as he puts it; 'it appears', he writes, 'that the connection between motives and voluntary actions is as regular and uniform as in any part of nature'. In addition, he introduced the idea of inference 'from character to conduct'.

Both ideas were accepted by Kant, who held that full psychological information would enable us to 'calculate in advance, and with certainty, as we do with a lunar or solar eclipse, any man's future behaviour'.[2] This statement shows his strong belief in 'scientific' determinism. The question is whether it is at all supported by psychological observations, such as Hume had in mind, on the regular conjunction between motives and actions.

Now I do not wish to deny the existence of psychological causes—of wishes, hopes, motives, and intentions; or of the feeling that a situation demands a certain action. On the contrary,

---

[1] Hobbes, *Quaestiones de libertate et necessitate, contra Doctorem Bramhallum*, 1656; Spinoza, *Ethics*, part I, prop. 32, corollary 2; part II, prop. 49, scholium (see especially the answer to the fourth objection); Hume, *Treatise*, 1739, book ii, sections i to iii; 'On Liberty and Necessity' (*Essays Moral, Political, and Literary*, 1742); J. Priestley, *The Doctrine of Philosophical Necessity*, 1777.

[2] *Critique of Practical Reason*, 4th to 6th eds., p. 172; or WW, ed. Cassirer, vol. 5, p. 108. The passage is quoted more fully in section 16 below.

I believe that there are many important cases in which physiological or physical causal explanations are bound to fail,[3] while at least something like a satisfactory psychological explanation may be given (or perhaps one in terms of the 'logic of the situation'[4]).

There are, for instance, good reasons for believing that in certain learning processes—in learning to walk, to talk, to write, to ski, to play the piano—there are physiological changes involved, such as, perhaps, the creation of characteristic nervous circuits; also that in practising what we have learned—in walking, or in talking—characteristic physiological reactions take place. But there is nothing to support the view that if a skier *invents* a *new* sequence of movements, or a writer a *new* sequence of words, or a composer a *new* sequence of chords, the physiological processes will be different from those in which the same sequences of movements or words or chords was (unconsciously) taken over from others. Of course, the invention of something new is often combined with a feeling of excitement which may have some physiological correlate; but in other cases, the innovator may be quite unconscious of his innovation, and unable to distinguish between what he has learned from others and what he has created himself.

It is important to realize, in this connection, that the fact that a certain achievement has the character of newness is a matter of interpretation and evaluation. To take an extreme example, somebody may apply a well-worn quotation in a situation which renders its use not only unexpected but creative and ingenious.

Appositeness, irony, and originality are then examples of qualities which may characterize a person's utterances and which should not be expected to be explicable in *physiological* terms. Yet there may be appropriate *psychological* explanations of the most diverse kind: the influence of the home atmosphere; examples and contacts which may have led to setting up unconscious

---

[3] *Cp.* the last paragraph of my paper 'Language and the Body-Mind Problem', *Proceedings of the XIth International Congress of Philosophy*, vol. vii, pp. 101 f. [Reprinted in *Conjectures and Refutations*, 1963, Chapter 12. Ed.]

[4] See my *Poverty of Historicism*, 1957, section 31, and *The Open Society and Its Enemies*, 1945, Chapter 14.

standards; reading, writing, and other educational influences may be used to explain such things. The invention of a new mathematical proof belongs here, and of new arguments; and perhaps even the attempt to follow an argument.

Thus there are few reasons for believing, and many for disbelieving, that a physiologist might be able to predict, from his study of a mathematician's brain, the steps of a new proof which the mathematician is about to invent. But once the proof is before us, we might find some *psychological* explanation for some of its steps: one might resemble an earlier proof by the same mathematician; another might be an ingenious application of a method invented by his teacher. A more penetrating analysis may even reveal some of the causes which made him think, in this particular situation, of his old teacher, and the kind of advice he may have received from him.

In all these cases, our causal explanation may be, in part or wholly, in terms of psychological hypotheses which can be tested by successful predictions. Thus we might have been able to predict successfully that Euler, faced with a problem of moderate difficulty, would be able to solve it; or that Mozart would compose a mass, or an opera, if he had accepted a commission to do so; and that, considering both his abilities and his conscientiousness, he would, in fact, produce a great work, and not merely something patched together for the occasion. There is no reason why we should not go further, and formulate testable and well-tested psychological hypotheses upon which predictions might be based—even predictions pertaining to new inventions.

These considerations of psychological 'causes' expose, I admit, a fundamental difficulty in the intuitive formulation of the doctrine of 'free will'. We shall hardly ever find a decision, an action, or new invention which is 'uncaused', in the sense that we could not 'causally explain' it in a satisfactory way, provided we knew a great deal, not only about the background, the wishes, the fears, and the attitudes of the person concerned, but also about the way in which his decisions may be influenced by arguments, or by his musical or literary tastes. Thus if the doctrine of 'free will' is meant to assert 'uncaused decisions' in this sense, then its criticism by Hobbes, Spinoza, Hume and their successors may be admitted to be sound.[5]

None of these considerations can be used, however, as arguments in favour of anything like 'scientific' determinism. For 'scientific' determinism asserts much more than the existence of causes. It asserts (as indicated in my quotation from Kant) that these causes allow us to predict an event with any desired degree of precision. It therefore involves the principle of accountability, that is to say, the possibility of calculating, from the prediction task, the degree of precision with which the 'causes'—i.e., the initial conditions—must be known, in order for the prediction problem to be solved.

But there is no reason whatever to believe that this principle can be satisfied in the field of the psychology of learning, or of motivation, any more than it can in that of behaviour or of physiology. On the contrary, there seems to be every reason for conjecturing that it will never be satisfied in the psychological field.

Kant's suggestion, for example, is clearly based upon a misunderstanding. It is based upon the mistaken belief that, if we can improve our knowledge of 'causes' indefinitely in some field, then we can also make our predictions in this field as precise as we wish. But this is clearly not generally true nor even plausible.

The idea of predicting, by psychological methods, a man's action with any desired degree of precision is indeed so completely foreign to all psychological thinking that it is hard to realize what it would entail. It would entail, for example, predicting with any desired degree of precision how fast a man will walk upstairs if he expects to find there a letter telling him that he has been promoted—or that he has been sacked. This would involve the combination of physical initial conditions of all kinds (the height of the stairs, the friction between shoes and

[5] I am assuming here that logical considerations such as, for example, our *realization* that two theories are interdeducible, or perhaps contradictory, may be looked upon as a 'cause'. See my 'Language and the Body-Mind Problem', *op.cit.*, esp. sections 6.1 to 6.4. [See also Popper's discussion of World 3 interaction with Worlds 1 and 2 in *The Self and Its Brain*, pp. 36–50. Ed.]

23

stairs), and of physiological initial conditions (the state of the man's general health, of his heart, of his lungs, etc.) with, for example, economic initial conditions (the man's savings, his chances of alternative employment, the number of people dependent on him), and psychological initial conditions (his self-confidence or anxiety, etc.). Nobody can say how these might be assessed, even if they were known; how they would have to be evaluated; and how the psychological conditions, more especially, could be used in such a way that they might be treated in the manner of the physical forces with which they would have to be compared and combined.

A psychoanalyst may, in many years of study (not a few analyses last for more than a decade), unearth all kinds of 'causes'—motives and what not—buried in his patient's unconscious. Let us assume that the analyst will be able, in a great number of cases, to predict his patient's behaviour successfully. Even so, few will believe that, with all his knowledge about his patient's motives, the analyst will be able to predict the exact time his patient will take, under varying psychological conditions, to walk up the stairs. The analyst may perhaps say that he would be able to make even this prediction if he were given sufficient data. *But he will not be able to state, and account for, what data would suffice for this purpose.* For there does not exist even a trace of a theory which would allow the analyst to calculate the degree of precision required of those data.

Psychological knowledge of a man (or a cat) may enable us to predict that he won't commit murder or theft (or that the cat won't bite or scratch). But in order to establish 'scientific' determinism, much more would be needed.

Once we realize what is implied by 'scientific' determinism—and especially by the principle of accountability—we see that psychological knowledge would also have to be supplemented by physiological knowledge, in exactly the same way as behavioural knowledge would have to be supplemented by physiological knowledge (as we saw when discussing the argument from behaviour). This means, of course, that the argument from psychology collapses.

Needless to say, the argument from psychology was from the beginning more vulnerable than the argument from behaviour. Not so much, I think, because we cannot measure the intensity of motives, for the behaviourist's measurements do not help him, as we have seen; but rather because the use of a concept such as 'motive', or 'character' is, as a little reflection shows, hardly more than a somewhat clumsy attempt to find law-like connections— or even to invent them when we cannot find them. I do not deny that a question like 'What was the motive of his action?' or a why-question such as 'Why did he do it?' may be perfectly reasonable; and so may be an answer like 'He did it out of jealousy (or from ambition, or for revenge)'. But all answers of this kind, even if they are highly sophisticated, are not much more than crude attempts to classify; or at best, to construct a hypothetical situational schema[6] which makes the action rationally understandable. They are throughout attempts to understand *post hoc;* this is so even in the rare cases when we operate with a schema that might be tested by confronting it with predictions.

8. *The Determinist Picture of the World.*

Neither the arguments from behaviour nor those from psychology are based upon experience: few people would assert that we have made many precise predictions in these fields. They seem to me, rather, to flow from the prior conviction that *the physical world* is deterministic. In a deterministic physical world, there is clearly no room for indeterministic behaviour; for all behaviour consists of events within the physical world. On the other hand, it might seem that there would be room for states of consciousness which are not determined. But the assumption that such states of consciousness exist would be highly unsatisfactory, and indeed gratuitous. They could have no kind of causal connection with behaviour. We could not know about them, or, at any rate, we should be unable to talk about them. For if we did, undeter-

---

[6] See the references in footnotes 3 and 4 above.

mined events would have some causal influence upon the physical world of sounds; an assumption which would contradict the doctrine that the physical world is deterministic.

In this way, a deterministic view of the physical world imposes upon us a deterministic view of the world of behaviour, and of the world of psychology; and indeed, Hobbes's and his successors' view of the physical world was deterministic. This does not prove, of course, that the argument from psychology which they put forward (or the argument from behaviour which was put forward by Hume and Schlick) was the result of this conviction: but it suggests that it was.

It is interesting to note that Hobbes's belief that the physical world was deterministic preceded Newton's theory. Newton's magnificent success thus could readily be interpreted as a most impressive corroboration of the determinist doctrine. It seemed that Newton had turned the old determinist programme into a reality.

This explains the strong reliance upon the truth of determinism which we find, for example, in Kant.

The suggestion that the arguments from behaviour and from psychology result from a deterministic view of the physical world would also explain why none of those who proposed these arguments ever stopped to consider the problem of accountability. For in a Hobbesian clockwork picture of the physical world, accountability seems intuitively obvious;[1] and so it does in the Newtonian picture (at least if we do not go too deeply into the details of the many-body problem). If the physical world were deterministic, and if accountability were satisfied in the field of physics, then there would be no need to worry about accountability in the fields of behaviour or psychology.

I believe that our discussion shows that the popular or commonsense arguments for determinism, as well as the traditional philosophical arguments, are invalid. But it also suggests that we can expect the strongest arguments to emerge from classical physics. But before turning to physics, I am going to

---

[1] Descartes's attempt to make room, in his clockwork picture of the world, for undetermined minds interfering with matter is unconvincing.

explain in a general way some reasons why indeterminism should be considered as *prima facie* acceptable, and why the burden of proof should rest upon the determinist.

9. *The Burden of Proof.*

An important reason for accepting indeterminism, at least tentatively, is that the burden of proof rests upon the shoulders of the determinist. The only reasonably strong arguments in favour of determinism known to me are those in favour of 'scientific' determinism; and in view of the fact that the commonsense arguments in favour of 'scientific' determinism all seem to break down when confronted with the problem of accountability, it seems that common sense is on balance in favour of indeterminism.

There are several reasons why the burden of proof seems to me to rest upon the determinist. I shall mention only four.

First, unsophisticated common sense favours the view that there are clocks *and* clouds, that is to say, events which are more predictable, and events which are less predictable; that predetermination and predictability are matters of degree.

Secondly, there is a *prima facie* case for the view that organisms are less predetermined and predictable than at least some simpler systems, and that the higher organisms are less predetermined and predictable than the lower ones.

Beavers (or men) produce characteristic and unmistakable changes in their physical environment. No doubt, the physical environment may reciprocate in producing characteristic and unmistakable changes in beavers (or in men). But in order to establish the truth of determinism, much more would have to be shown. Assuming that beavers have not always existed, the determinist would have to show that physical conditions (other than the presence of beavers) can produce, in a predictable way, beavers. But although we know a great deal about physical conditions produced by beavers, we certainly know nothing about any physical conditions which may produce beavers. Here is an asymmetry in our knowledge, and the burden of proving that the gap in our knowledge can be filled rests upon the determinist; up till now, he has at best a programme.

A third reason, and one which I think most important, is closely related to the 'free will' problem. If determinism is true, it should in principle be possible for a physicist or a physiologist who knows nothing of music to predict, by studying Mozart's brain, the spots on the paper on which he will put down his pen. Beyond this, the physicist or physiologist should be able to anticipate Mozart's action and write his symphony even before it is consciously conceived by Mozart. Analogous results would hold for mathematical discoveries, and all other additions to our knowledge. In spite of the fact that a man like Kant was implicitly committed to uphold these results, they appear to me intuitively as absurd. Absurd or not, they go far beyond anything known to us; thus, again, the burden of proof rests upon the determinist.

Fourthly, indeterminism, which asserts that there exists *at least one* event that is not predetermined, or predictable, is clearly a weaker assertion than 'scientific' determinism, which asserts that all events are in principle predictable. Although I prefer, within science, stronger theories to weaker ones, I do so because they are better arguable, that is to say, criticizable. In any case, he who proposes the stronger theory accepts the burden of proof: he must produce arguments in favour of his theory—mainly by exhibiting its explanatory power. But determinism, even its version which I call 'scientific', does not belong to science, and has no explanatory power.

CHAPTER II

'SCIENTIFIC' DETERMINISM

10. Prima Facie *Determinism of Classical Physics. Laplace's Demon*.

Quantum physicists often say that what they call 'classical physics' (this comprises Newton's, Maxwell's and even Einstein's theories) implies determinism, while quantum physics implies indeterminism. Without admitting the truth of this remark, I am willing, of course, to admit that there is a difference between classical and quantum physics. Quantum theory is a probability theory, while classical physics has a different character.[1] I propose to describe classical physics as *'prima facie* deterministic', indicating by this name that I do not wish to prejudice the issue whether or not it entails some kind of determinism.

What I call the *'prima facie* deterministic character' of classical physics may best be described with the help of the so-called 'Laplacean demon'.

Laplace believed that the world consists of corpuscles acting upon one another according to Newtonian dynamics, and that a complete and precise knowledge of the initial state of the world system at one instant of time should suffice for the deduction of its state at any other instant. (The 'state' of a Newtonian system is given if the complete initial conditions, i.e., the positions, masses, velocities and directions of the movement, of all its

---

[1] There are theories which fall into neither of these two categories, especially all qualitative and classificatory theories.

29

particles are given.[2]) Knowledge of this kind is clearly superhuman. This is why Laplace introduced the fiction of a demon—a superhuman intelligence, capable of ascertaining the complete set of initial conditions of the world system at any one instant of time. With the help of these initial conditions and the laws of nature, i.e., the equations of mechanics, the demon would be able, according to Laplace, to deduce all future states of the world system; this showed that, provided the laws of nature are known, the future of the world is implicit in any instant of its past; and so, the truth of determinism would be established.[3]

The crucial point about this argument of Laplace's is this. *It makes the doctrine of determinism a truth of science rather than of religion.* Laplace's demon is not an omniscient God, merely a super-scientist. He is not supposed to be able to do anything which human scientists could not do, or at least approximately do: he merely is supposed to be able to carry out his tasks with superhuman perfection.

Thus Laplace would have been ready to admit that human scientists cannot ascertain the initial conditions of all the physical bodies in the universe; but he would have pointed out that they can measure all the initial conditions of a solar system if the number of planets is small. He would also have been ready to admit that scientists cannot obtain absolutely exact initial conditions; but he would have pointed out that they can improve the degree of precision in measuring them, and that there is no absolute limit to these improvements. Again, he would have admitted that, if the system contains more than two bodies, Newton's theory allows us to calculate the future state of the system only by a method of approximation, according to our present state of mathematical knowledge; but Laplace would have pointed out that, though we have not solved the general many-body problem—i.e., the problem of calculating the Newtonian gravitational interaction of more than two bodies—we

[2] With respect to field theories, it should be understood that the 'initial conditions' of the system (in my sense) include boundary conditions.

[3] [See P. S. Laplace: *Essai philosophique sur les probabilités*, 1819, Introduction. See also Popper: *The Self and Its Brain*, p. 22. Ed.]

might one day find its solution, which certainly would make it legitimate to invest the demon with this knowledge; and he might have added that, even though the general problem might be strictly insoluble, we can, in every *particular* case (provided it is not too complex), replace the exact solution by an approximation which is precise to any degree we may choose to stipulate.

It is in this sense that Laplace's demon is only an idealized human scientist. Actually, he is an idealized Laplace. Laplace believed that he had solved the great problem of the stability of our own solar system. He believed that he had proved—under the assumption that the system was closed, i.e., that no new body would enter it or interfere with it from outside—that the planets would *in all future periods of time* continue to keep their present mean distances from the sun. (We shall see in sections 12 and 14 that he was mistaken.)

Laplace's demon is supposed to work, like a human scientist, with initial conditions and with *theories*, i.e., systems of natural laws. Theories which for appropriate physical systems fully answer his purpose may be labelled '*prima facie* deterministic'.

This label is introduced here in order to characterize certain features of Newton's or Maxwell's or Einstein's theories in contradistinction to other theories, such as thermodynamics, or statistical mechanics, or quantum theory, and perhaps also the theory of genes. I suggest the following definition.

A physical theory is *prima facie* deterministic if and only if it allows us to deduce, from a *mathematically exact* description of the initial state of a closed physical system which is described in terms of the theory, the description, *with any stipulated finite degree of precision*, of the state of the system at any given future instant of time.

This definition does not demand mathematically exact predictions, even though the initial conditions are assumed to be mathematically absolutely exact. We cannot demand more, if we wish to make sure that Newton's mechanics is not excluded by the definition, since only approximate methods are known for the solution of the problem of more than two bodies.

31

It may even be argued that, for similar reasons, we ought to weaken our definition by adding the words 'provided the physical system in question is not too complex'. For it is not known whether satisfactory methods exist of solving many-body problems by approximation when the system in question contains very many bodies, and especially if the masses and the distances of the bodies are all of the same order of magnitude. The point is, of course, that even with mathematically exact initial conditions, the methods of numerical computation introduce imprecisions of their own which, in the case of some complex systems, we may be unable to reduce, by successive steps of approximation, below a certain level.[4] Thus it may be impossible to obtain a prediction of any desired degree of precision.

Although this point is important, I shall not pursue it here; on the contrary, I shall *assume*—as a concession to my determinist opponents—that Newton's and Maxwell's theories are *prima facie* deterministic in the sense of my original definition.

Having adopted this definition, the question before us is the following. Assuming that a *prima facie* deterministic physical theory is *true,* are we entitled to infer from this assumption the truth of 'scientific' determinism? Or in other words, are we entitled to infer the deterministic character of the world from the *prima facie* deterministic character of a theory?

I shall later (in section 13) give various reasons why I believe that this inference would be invalid. But my next task is to explain more clearly the idea of 'scientific' determinism.

11. *The Idea of 'Scientific' Determinism: Predictability from Within.*

The general idea of determinism may be explained, as we have seen, with the help of the metaphor of a film showing successive states of the world. In this film, what will be shown in the future is as fixed, or determined, as what has been shown in the past. And since the future is fixed, it might, in principle, be foreknown; not merely guessed, but foreknown with certainty.

[4] See also J. von Neumann and H. H. Goldstine, 'Numerical Inverting of Matrices of High Order', *Bull. Am. Math. Soc.* **53**, 1947, pp. 1022–99.

Keeping this metaphor in mind, we might say that 'scientific' determinism results from the attempt to replace the vague idea of possible foreknowledge by the more precise idea of *predictability in accordance with rational scientific procedures of prediction*. That is, it asserts that the future can be *rationally deduced*, from present or past initial conditions, in conjunction with true universal theories.

It is important to realize that 'scientific' determinism asserts more than the mere possibility, or even the existence, of fore-knowledge, and that it therefore lends itself more readily to criticism. Clearly, it is logically possible that every event may be foreknown by somebody (who dreams it, for example, in advance), even in a world in which many events happen in a haphazard fashion, and are not subject to anything like universal laws. In such a world, 'scientific' determinism would be false, since there would be no true theories sufficiently strong to be used as a basis for rational scientific prediction. We can express this by saying that 'scientific' determinism asserts more than the motion-picture character of the world. It asserts that the events shown in the film are never haphazard but always subject to rules, so that each picture or shot belonging to the film allows us to *calculate by rational methods* any of those which follow, with the help of the rules or laws connecting successive shots. Unless it implies this much, a determinist doctrine will not be of the 'scientific' type.

What has been said may perhaps clarify the relation between the general idea of determinism and that version of it which I have labelled 'scientific'. The crucial point is that the latter appeals to *the success of human science*, such as Newtonian theory: 'scientific' determinism is to appear as a result of the success of empirical science, or at least as supported by it. It appears to be based upon *human experience*.

This was no doubt why Laplace appealed not to an omniscient God, but merely to a demon vested with powers which, he intended, should not *in principle* surpass those of the human scientist. Laplace did not expect his demon to know any future state of the world by intuition; this would not idealize human rational powers but would in principle go beyond them. Laplace did, however, expect his demon to know initial conditions precisely, no doubt because he believed that there were no limits to the possible improvement of human knowledge in this direction. Similarly, he expected his demon to know the condition of *all* corpuscles in a system of any degree of complexity; again, no doubt, because he believed there was no limit to human knowledge in this respect, even though he realized that no human being (or no computer of any given finite size) could ever, in practice, find out the co-ordinates of all the corpuscles in a system like a gas which contains a very great number of them. We may, perhaps, best express Laplace's intention by saying that the demon's powers were to exceed those of the human scientist only in degree; they were to be unlimited only in fields where there were *no definite limits* to the human scientist's powers.

This idea may be made more precise with the help of two important requirements to which Laplace undoubtedly would have agreed. These two requirements, formulated here with reference to the demon, will later, in a slightly more abstract form, be incorporated in our final definition of 'scientific' determinism.

The first requirement is as follows.

(1) The demon, like a human scientist, must *not* be assumed to be able *to ascertain initial conditions with absolute mathematical precision*; like a human scientist, he will have to be content with a finite degree of precision. But it may be assumed that the demon can make the range of imprecision of his measurements as small as he likes, i.e., smaller than any finite range which anybody may specify.

At first sight this requirement seems to amount to no more than a minor adjustment of our definition of a *prima facie* deterministic theory; for we have called a theory *prima facie* deterministic that allows us to calculate any prediction, with any desired, or specified, degree of precision, if we are given *mathematically exact* initial conditions. The doctrine of 'scientific' determinism requires a little more: that we—or the demon—should be able to calculate any prediction with any desired, or specified, degree of precision if we are given initial conditions of a *finite degree of imprecision* (provided always that the imprecision does not exceed a degree which we may stipulate in advance, on the basis of the prediction task, in accordance with the principle of accountability).

The second requirement is as follows.

(2) The demon, like a human scientist, must be assumed to belong himself to the physical world whose future he is to predict; at least it must be assumed that *physical* processes exist in the world which may be interpreted (a) as processes by which the demon may obtain information, (b) as processes of calculating the prediction, and (c) as processes of formulating the prediction. In other words, the demon must be visualized not as a disembodied spirit, outside the physical system which he is to predict, but rather as the physical incarnation of a spirit, as it were: his essential activities must, in some way, interact with the system. We may sum up this requirement by saying that he must *predict the system from within*, rather than from without.

This second demand is again derivable from the requirement that the demon must not be vested with powers which *in principle* surpass all human powers. This is no *ad hoc* demand of mine. It has been tacitly assumed by physicists, for thirty years at least, to be part of the doctrine of determinism. This becomes apparent when certain arguments of Heisenberg's are remembered, arguments to which I may refer here without thereby accepting them.[1] I am alluding to the argument that determinism will not do in view of the fact that, due to the interference of the process of measuring with the state of the measured system, there are

[1] I do not agree with these ideas of Heisenberg's. I feel that I should say this here quite bluntly since in my paper 'Indeterminism in Quantum Physics and in Classical Physics', in which I first formulated what is here presented as demand (2), I sometimes spoke as if I accepted the idea that quantum indeterminism is due to the interference of the measuring process with the objects measured. This way of speaking was due, I suppose, to the fact that when writing that paper, my aim was not to criticize quantum physics but rather to show that certain characteristics believed to be peculiar to it apply also to classical physics. [See Popper: 'Quantum Mechanics without "The Observer"', reprinted as the Introduction to *Quantum Theory and the Schism in Physics*, Vol. III of the *Postscript*. Ed.]

definite limits to the possible precision of our knowledge of the initial conditions, and therefore to the predictions which can be calculated from them. This argument amounts to rejecting the idea that the demon may be a disembodied spirit: it assumes that the demon is not to be vested with unlimited powers where limits would in principle apply to any human being and to any physical instrument. In other words, Heisenberg's argument against determinism is based upon the implicit assumption that determinism entails *predictability from within,* with any desired degree of precision.

12. *Two Definitions of 'Scientific' Determinism.*

We can now define 'scientific' determinism as follows:

The doctrine of 'scientific' determinism is *the doctrine that the state of any closed physical system at any given future instant of time can be predicted, even from within the system, with any specified degree of precision, by deducing the prediction from theories, in conjunction with initial conditions whose required degree of precision can always be calculated (in accordance with the principle of accountability) if the prediction task is given.*

This is *the weakest definition* which is yet strong enough to formulate the ideas involved in a 'scientific' determinism.

What our definition demands is the predictability of *any* event, by demanding (as indicated in previous sections) predictability of the state of *any* physical system, at any given future time, with *any* specified degree of precision. In addition, it incorporates the demands (1) and (2) explained in the preceding section, and also the principle of accountability. All these are indispensable ingredients of the idea of 'scientific' determinism.

On the other hand, *stronger* definitions could be given: there are possible ingredients of the idea of 'scientific' determinism which some may feel, intuitively, to be essential parts of it, and which are omitted from our definition. I have in mind, more especially, the idea that we can predict of any system *whether or not an event of a given kind will ever occur in it.* In other words, we might add, to the definition just given, the requirement that it can be predicted, of any given state, *whether or not the system in question will ever be in this state.*

If this requirement is added to our definition, we obtain what we may call *the stronger version of 'scientific' determinism.* The question whether there will ever occur a solar eclipse (or, say, a solar eclipse followed within a fortnight by a lunar one), is an example which those may have in mind who consider the stronger version as essential to 'scientific' determinism. Another example, more important for our discussion, is the question studied by Laplace, whether or not our solar system is stable; or in a more concrete formulation, whether the mean distance between the sun and any planet will ever be, say, twice their present mean distance, or half of it.

It was, partly, his belief that he had solved this problem which suggested to Laplace the idea of the demon. Thus it might be said that the stronger version is very near to the one Laplace had in mind.

13. *Does 'Scientific' Determinism follow from a* Prima Facie Deterministic Theory?

At first sight, it may seem that the definition of 'scientific' determinism, even in its stronger version, is so closely similar to that of a *prima facie* deterministic theory that the truth of 'scientific' determinism would immediately follow from the truth of any *prima facie* deterministic theory, such as Newton's mechanics. This impression no doubt explains why not only Kant and Laplace but so many other great thinkers who firmly believed in the truth of Newton's mechanics thought that they were bound to accept some such doctrine as 'scientific' determinism. Einstein too believed in the validity of the inference,[1] and so did his opponents, the defenders of the official interpretation of quantum theory (the 'Copenhagen interpretation'). And yet, the inference is invalid.

[1] [But see Chapter I, footnote 2, above, which suggests that Einstein abandoned the idea. Ed.]

37

First, it should be realized that there is a considerable difference between what I have called the *prima facie* deterministic character of a theory, and 'scientific' determinism. In asserting the first, we always assert *of a theory* that it has a certain property. In asserting the second, we assert *of the world* that it has a certain property. Admittedly, if a theory is true, then it describes certain properties of the world. But this does not mean that for every property of a true theory, there will be a corresponding property of the world.

To give a first indication that it may be dangerous to rely on the impression that 'scientific' determinism follows from the *prima facie* deterministic character of a theory, the following should be remembered. Even if we were to assume that Newton's mechanics is true, it would be clear that he had not yet obtained a theory entailing 'scientific' determinism, if for no other reason than because not all physical events had been shown by him to be mechanical; only after a successful deduction from Newton's mechanics of a satisfactory theory of electricity, of magnetism, and of optics, could the question arise whether or not the truth of Newton's mechanics may be used as an argument for 'scientific' determinism. Or in other words, 'scientific' determinism could, if at all, follow only from a system of physics which was *complete, or comprehensive,* in the sense that it would allow the prediction of all kinds of physical events.[2]

A second warning against relying on the impression that 'scientific' determinism follows from the truth of a *prima facie* deterministic theory may be derived from the fact that *the stronger version,* at any rate, of 'scientific' determinism is false, even if we assume that the world is a purely mechanical system (without electricity, etc.) and that Newton's mechanics is true. This will be shown in the next section, with the help of a result of Hadamard's. Later I shall try to show more; not only that even the weaker version of 'scientific' determinism is incompatible

[2] Kant and Laplace, it should be remembered, flourished just at that period of the history of science (1785–1818) when there was more reason than in any other to believe that the programme of reducing all physics to Newton's mechanics was one likely to succeed.

with certain theories—for example, Einstein's—but also that it must be rejected on logical grounds.

14. *A Result of Hadamard's.*

In a very interesting paper,[1] published in 1898, Hadamard discussed a simple mechanical problem: the movement, with constant velocity, of a mass-point along the geodesics—i.e., the straightest lines—of an infinite curved surface (of a special kind, viz. with varying negative curvature; it is assumed that there are no discontinuities). Hadamard assumes that the initial position (the starting point of the movement) is given with absolute precision; and he allows the initial direction of the movement to vary within an angle α. He shows that there will then be several *kinds of tracks,* especially (i) *orbits or closed tracks,* including curves which are only asymptotically closed such that a point moving on them will always remain within a finite distance from the starting point, and (ii) *trajectories going to infinity,* such that, after a sufficiently long period of time, a point moving on them will exceed any given finite distance from the starting point.[2] We consider two different orbits (closed tracks) issuing from our starting point at two different initial directions enclosing a small angle α. Hadamard shows that, even if we make α as small as we like, there will nevertheless be tracks *going to infinity* which issue from our starting point *within* the angle α; that is to say, between any two different *orbits* we may choose.

But this means that no measurement of the initial *direction* of the track, however precise (short of absolute mathematical precision) can determine whether the mass-point is moving on an orbit, or else on a trajectory that eventually goes to infinity; not even on the unrealistic assumption that the initial *position* is given with absolute precision. It means, in other words, that we cannot determine whether the mass-point will move in such a way that its

---

[1] J. Hadamard, '*Les surfaces à courbures opposées*', etc., *Journal des Mathématiques pures et appliquées*, 5th series, vol. **4**, 1898, pp. 27–73; see also Pierre Duhem, *The Aim and Structure of Physical Theory*, p. 139 *ff*.

[2] Hadamard distinguishes a third category of geodesics—the borderline cases—which need not concern us here.

distance from the starting point never exceeds a finite value, or whether it will eventually begin to increase its distance steadily, and move off to infinity.

Thus the stronger version of 'scientific' determinism discussed in the preceding section is refuted by Hadamard's results. For, as Hadamard points out,[3] no finite degree of precision of the initial conditions will allow us to predict whether or not a planetary system (of many bodies) will be stable in Laplace's sense. This is due to the fact that mathematically exact initial states which determine orbits, and others which determine geodesics going to infinity, cannot, as we have seen, be disentangled by any physical measurements. With this, Hadamard refutes Laplace's result (mentioned above); a result which may well have been one of the main inspirations of Laplace's idea of 'scientific' determinism.

However, Hadamard does not, as far as I can see, refute the weaker doctrine of 'scientific' determinism, as I have defined it above. We can still obtain predictions, *for any given* instant of time, of the state of the mass-point, provided we measure its initial direction with a degree of precision which will depend upon (a) the time span between the start and the instant mentioned in the prediction task, and (b) the degree of precision specified in the prediction. What we *cannot* predict is the behaviour of the system *for all* instants of time.[4]

---

[3] *Loc. cit.*, p. 71 (section 59). Hadamard says there that his results suggest that the problem of stability of the solar system 'would cease to have any sense'. I disagree. To show that a prediction problem cannot be calculated on the basis of any theory, and any measurement of the initial conditions, however precise, does not render the problem meaningless at all; rather, it establishes that it is insoluble. An insoluble problem is not a meaningless one, and the discovery of its insolubility may elucidate it just as much as the discovery of a solution.

[4] The difference between 'for all' and 'for any given', in this formulation, shows a certain analogy to the fact (discovered by Gödel) that although we can construct for any given arithmetical statement a formalized theory in which the statement is decidable, we cannot construct a formalized theory in which all arithmetical statements are decidable. With this analogy in mind, we may say that an Hadamardian question (which asks whether a many-body system whose initial conditions are given with any finite degree of precision will ever be in some specified state) is a *physically undecidable question*.

CHAPTER III

THE CASE FOR INDETERMINISM

15. *Why I am an Indeterminist: Theories as Nets.*

I personally believe that the doctrine of indeterminism is true, and that determinism is completely baseless.

Outstanding among the reasons for my conviction is the intuitive argument (mentioned in section 7 above) that the creation of a new work, such as Mozart's G minor symphony, cannot be predicted, in all its details, by a physicist, or physiologist, who studies in detail Mozart's body—especially his brain—and his physical environment. The opposite view seems intuitively absurd; at any rate, it seems obvious that it would be most difficult to produce reasonable arguments in its favour, and that there is at present nothing whatever except a quasi-religious prejudice to support it or the prejudice that the omniscience of science somehow approaches, if only in principle, divine omniscience.

I frankly admit that this point is closely connected with the traditional problem of 'free will' which, however, I am not going to discuss. The problem which interests me here, rather, is the one which arises in our example about Mozart—whether the world is such that we could in principle, if only we knew enough, predict even unique events such as the creation of a new symphony in every detail, by the rational methods of science. This is the only problem which interests me in this field. I must make this quite clear, because I am merely bored by the analysis of the meaning of the words 'free' and 'will', and by the question whether Mozart or anybody else could have done otherwise than he did. I am interested in the world of facts; and although since Schlick (who introduced meaning analysis into this field, under the influence of Wittgenstein), it has been widely accepted that even Hume was concerned with the analysis of the meaning of words, this is, in my view, a misunderstanding.[1] I do not doubt that Hume too was interested in the structure of the world, and that he cleared up verbal misunderstandings only where he thought them to be obstacles to an understanding of the world.

It is thus the alleged scientific predictability of unique achievements which interests me, and which I find utterly unbelievable. It is one of those questions, a few of which were enumerated in section 9, where the burden of proof rests upon the determinist.

But it is not enough to burden the determinist with the responsibility of providing arguments for often repeated assertions which seem to me wild, and for which no good arguments have ever been offered. There are also strong philosophical arguments, partly logical and partly metaphysical, *against* determinism; arguments which, many years ago, convinced me of the weakness of 'scientific' determinism.[2]

I see our scientific theories as human inventions—nets designed by us to catch the world. To be sure, these differ from the inventions of the poets, and even from the inventions of the technicians. Theories are not *only* instruments. What we aim at is truth: we test our theories in the hope of eliminating those which are not true. In this way we may succeed in improving our theories—even as instruments: in making nets which are better and better adapted to catch our fish, the real world. Yet they will never be perfect instruments for this purpose. They are rational nets of our own making, and should not be mistaken for a complete representation of the real world in all its aspects; not

[1] See especially Schlick's *Fragen der Ethik*, 1930, chapter vii, section 1, pp. 105 *ff*.

[2] It so happens that my first published essay ('Über die Stellung des Lehrers zu Schule und Schüler', in *Schulreform* 4, 1925, pp. 204–8) was devoted to fundamentally the same argument as that developed in what follows here.

even if they are highly successful; not even if they appear to yield excellent approximations to reality.[3]

If we keep clearly before our minds that our theories are our own work; that we are fallible; and that our theories reflect our fallibility, then we shall doubt whether general features of our theories, such as their simplicity, or their *prima facie* deterministic character, correspond to features of the real world.

What I mean is this. If we have tested a statement like 'All dogs have tails', and it has stood up to our tests, then perhaps all dogs (or cats) have tails, or at least approximately all. But it would be a mistake to conclude from the fact that such a universalized subject-predicate sentence has been found to be fairly successful in describing the world, or even from the fact that it is true, that the world has a subject-predicate structure, or that it consists of substances having certain properties. Similarly, the success, or even the truth, of simple statements, or of mathematical statements, or of English statements, ought not to tempt us to draw the inference that the world is intrinsically simple, or mathematical, or British.[4] All these inferences have in fact been drawn by some philosopher or other; but upon reflection, there is little to recommend them. The world, as we know it, is highly complex; and although it may possess structural aspects which are simple in some sense or other, the simplicity of some of our theories—which is of our own making—does not entail the intrinsic simplicity of the world.

The situation with regard to determinism is similar. Newton's theory, consisting of the law of inertia, the law of gravity, etc., may be true, or very approximately true, i.e., the world may be as the theory asserts it is. But there is no statement of determinism in this theory; the theory nowhere asserts that the world is determined; rather it is the *theory itself* which has that character which I have called '*prima facie* deterministic'.

[3] *Cp.* J. von Neumann and H. H. Goldstine, *op. cit.*, p. 1024: 'This . . . is . . . closely related to the methodological observation that a mathematical formulation necessarily represents only a (more or less explicit) theory of some phase (or aspect) of reality, and not reality itself.'

[4] *Cp.* my paper 'What is Dialectic?', *Mind* 49, N.S., p. 414, esp. p. 420, reprinted in *Conjectures and Refutations*, pp. 312–35, esp. p. 330.

Now the *prima facie* deterministic character of a theory is closely related to its simplicity; *prima facie* deterministic theories are comparatively easily testable, and the tests may be made more and more precise and severe. It follows from my considerations on content, testability, and simplicity, that theories of this kind should be preferred to others; which is why we try to construct them in preference to others, and to stick to them (if they stand up to tests) wherever the problems before us permit.[5] At the same time, it seems no more justifiable to infer from their success that the world has an intrinsically deterministic character than to infer that the world is intrinsically simple.

The method of science depends upon our attempts to describe the world with simple theories: theories that are complex may become untestable, even if they happen to be true. Science may be described as the art of systematic over-simplification—the art of discerning what we may with advantage omit.

It is important to see the connection between this result and the problem of accountability. Consider a prediction task such as the calculation of the state of our solar system three months hence, with a stipulated precision of the final positions and of the final momenta of the planets. If in the sense of accountability we wish to calculate the permissible imprecision of the initial conditions, then we need not only Newton's mechanics but also a *model* of our solar system. In other words, we need a list of the planets, of their masses, positions, and velocities; that is, we need an approximate description of the state of the system today. But in giving this description, we must invariably make use of our theory.

First, it is the theory which decides what belongs to the state of the system (positions, masses, velocities) and what does not (for example, the diameters of the planets; their temperatures; their thermal capacities; and their chemical and magnetic properties).

Secondly, the theory tells us what size of 'planets' may be neglected (meteorites, for example). In other words, it is altogether naïve to think of 'every prediction task' as if it meant

[5] *Cf. L.Sc.D.*, end of section 36.

every conceivable state of the world, or event in the world: every prediction task, and especially every prediction task which may conceivably be accountable, operates with a simplifying *model*. It is the result of seeing the world in the light of a simplifying theory; and whatever is not illuminated by this searchlight remains obscure: it is neglected.[6]

The universality of our theories raises similar problems. We have much reason to believe that the world is unique: a unique and highly complex—perhaps even infinitely complex— combination of occurrences of interacting processes. Yet we try to describe this unique world with the help of *universal* theories. Do these theories describe universal features of the world, regularities? Or is universality, like simplicity, a characteristic merely of our theories—perhaps of our theoretical language—but not of the world?

I believe that the case here is somewhat different from that of simplicity. If we say 'All dogs have tails', then we do in fact assert something about all dogs; this is clear because we may have to retract the statement if we find a tailless race of dogs (analogous to the tailless race of Manx cats). Thus universality is something which our theories assert, and something which we set out to test. Simplicity, on the other hand, is not asserted by our theories; and if it were, we might not know how to test it.[7]

At the same time, it is just our attempt to *explain* the world, i.e., to describe it in terms of ever more universal theories, which leads us up the ladder, not only of levels of universality, but also of levels of approximation. The theories we supersede by ex-

---

[6] [*(Added 1981)   I have in several places spoken of the 'searchlight theory of science' (*Open Society*, vol. ii, pp. 260–262, 361; *Objective Knowledge*, Appendix I; *Conjectures and Refutations*, pp. 127f.). More recently, I have also spoken of the 'searchlight theory of human language', in connection with the problem formulated in *Conjectures* on pp. 213f. The point of the metaphor is that the searchlight *may* illuminate some aspect of the world (even from a chosen position) without influencing it or in any way interfering with it: the objectivity of the truth of a statement may be absolute, even though the fact it describes cannot be abstracted (or picked out) from reality except with the help of human descriptive language.]

[7] *Cp.* also *L.Sc.D.*, section 15, and Appendix *vii.

plaining them with the help of theories of higher universality often appear, from the new level, only as approximations.

It is conceivable that this process of approximation may come to an end one day, for the reason that we may one day arrive at *the* true and complete theory of the world (although at the present time this day looks far away—much farther than it looked at the time of Kant and Laplace). But even if we should find the true theory of the world, we could not—as Xenophanes realized[8]—possibly know that we had found it. For nearly two centuries, Newton's theory was held to be *the* true theory of the world; and even if we find a theory which appears to us to be as satisfactory as Newton's theory appeared to most physicists during these two centuries, we ought never to feel sure that some serious objection to it might not be found some day.

Thus we should not dismiss the possibility that we may have to be content with improving our approximations for ever. It may well be a consequence of *the uniqueness of the world* that the attempt to describe it in terms of universal theories leads to an infinite sequence of approximations, not unlike the attempt to describe an irrational number in terms of ratios of natural numbers.[9] Our attempt to describe the world in terms of universal theories may be an attempt to rationalize the unique, the irrational, in terms of our self-made universal laws.[10] (It

[8] See Diels-Krantz, 21 [11], Fragment 34 (6th edition, 1951, p. 137). [See also Popper: 'Back to the Presocratics', in *Conjectures and Refutations*, pp. 136–65, esp. pp. 152–3. Ed.]

[9] It is interesting to note that J.B.S. Haldane, starting essentially from the premise that our laws (or other 'laws which can, in principle, be formulated mathematically') are not only approximations but strictly true, arrives at the conclusion that our world is not unique, but repetitive—so that, for example 'every two persons who meet in the present life . . . will therefore do so an infinite number of times'. (See 'Consequences of Materialism', in *The Inequality of Man*, 1932, Pelican Books, 1937, pp. 169 and 168.) These speculations are, in Haldane's own eyes, 'strange' (p. 170); and their strangely metaphysical character may be appealed to in order to support the very opposite and I think less fantastic metaphysics—the theory of the uniqueness of the world, and the approximate character of all theories.

[10] With the view that the world is irrational, and that it is the task of science to rationalize it, compare note 19 to chapter 24 of my *Open Society*.

differs from the method of approximation by a sequence of ratios in that each step of approximation seems to describe a *partial aspect* of the world without which we could not understand the next.) Our very method of over-simplification may create the gap which we try to close by our approximations. But since there is no absolute measure for the degree of approximation achieved—for the coarseness or fineness of our net—but only a comparison with worse or better approximations, even our most successful efforts may produce only a net whose mesh is too coarse for determinism. We try to examine the world exhaustively by our nets; but its mesh will always let some small fish escape: there will always be enough play for indeterminism.

This may be seen most clearly where it concerns us most. There is no sign whatever that with the help of scientific methods we can approach anywhere near to a scientific description or classification of human personalities: they remain unique, in spite of all attempts at classification and measurement.

16. *Comparison with Kant's View.*

Most of the considerations advanced in the foregoing section are of a logical or methodological character. But the view of the uniqueness of the world may well be described as metaphysical: it corresponds closely to Kant's idea of the world of *noumena* or *things in themselves.*

Kant not only believed, like most of his contemporaries—astronomers and physicists included—in the truth of Newton's theory; he even believed that it was *a priori* valid.[1] The possibility that Newton's theory was only a splendid approximation did not,

---

[1] See especially Kant's *Metaphysical Foundations of Natural Science*, 1786 (published in the year before the second edition of the *Critique of Pure Reason*). It is, of course, well known that Kant was a Newtonian; it is not so well known—although it is of crucial significance for the understanding of his philosophy—that when he spoke of 'pure natural science', he meant Newtonian dynamics which he believed to be *a priori* valid. (See my paper on 'The Nature of Philosophical Problems and Their Roots in Science', *The British Journal for the Philosophy of Science* 3, 1952, esp. pp. 153 *ff.*, and 'Immanuel Kant—Philosopher of the Enlightenment', *The Listener*, February 18th, 1954.) [See *Conjectures and Refutations*, Chapters 2, 7, and 8. Ed.]

and I think, could not, occur to him. This is why he distinguished the world of appearance, or '*Nature*'—the world upon which our intellect imposes, *a priori*, its (Newtonian) laws—from the world of things in themselves, the real world of *noumena*. Nature, the world in space and time, was subject to causal laws, he believed; laws which determined everything in nature 'with necessity'. Our actions in space and time were completely predetermined; they could be calculated in advance, like eclipses. Only as *noumena*, as things in ourselves, could we be free.

If we replace Kant's world of *noumena* by our world of things or processes considered under the aspect of their uniqueness, and Kant's world of phenomena by our world of things considered under the aspect of universality, we come close to the view developed in the foregoing section; except that, as I have shown, causality has to be distinguished from determinism, and our world of uniqueness is—unlike Kant's noumenal world—in space and, even more important, in time; for I find it crucially important to distinguish between the determined *past* and the open *future*.

Thus I agree with Kant when he implies that a theory like Newton's is of our own making—imposed, as he puts it, by our intellect upon nature; that, in this way, our intellect rationalizes nature; and that there is a reality—deeper than that described by Newton's theory or any other theory—which we should not regard as deterministic. But I disagree with Kant's belief that Newton's theory must be true, and that a theory which we impose upon nature must for that reason be *a priori* valid, or of a *prima facie* deterministic character. I also disagree with his view that indeterminist reality itself cannot be known. Though the unique world in which we live can never be known completely, our scientific knowledge is an attempt—and a surprisingly successful attempt—to know it better and better. In this sense of knowledge, all our knowledge concerns only this one unique world of ours, and no other.

The fundamental difficulty of Kant's solution—that as free things in themselves, we are not in space and time, while our actions are in space and time and therefore determined—clearly does not arise in my solution. Thus it becomes possible to say that we are making moral decisions here and now (which, I do not doubt, Kant would have wished to be able to say).

Kant expresses his determinism in the following passage:[2]

'Thus we may admit the truth of the view that we could calculate in advance and with certainty—as we do with lunar or solar eclipses—any man's future behaviour, had we so deep an insight into his ways of thinking as to know all of his most intimate springs of action, as well as all the relevant external circumstances: and yet, at the same time, we may assert that man is free.'

This passage testifies to the power of Kant's belief in indeterminism: it was even stronger than his erroneous belief that science (*a priori* science) forced us to accept determinism. For what he says here of predictability is clearly pure determinism, as he himself emphasizes. Of course, his formula may be saved very simply by the remark that we can never have 'so deep an insight' as would be needed for the prediction task. But though this would save his formula, by vacuously satisfying it, it would not save what he intended to say; moreover, it would amount to abandoning accountability, and with it, 'scientific' determinism.

17. *Is Classical Physics Accountable?*

The philosophical arguments developed in section 15 and compared with those of Kant in the foregoing section suggest some results of a slightly more technical nature: they suggest a way of showing that classical physics is not accountable, even independently of Hadamard's decisive results.

The significance of these results is severely limited. They need not affect the deterministic or even the mechanistic picture of the world cherished by a Newtonian. They may be perfectly valid, and yet not surprise or shock a Newtonian. But they do affect 'scientific' determinism; that is to say, the view that determinism

[2] *Critique of Practical Reason*, 4th to 6th editions, p. 172. WW, ed. Cassirer, vol. 5, p. 108. See also note 2 in section 7 above.

is backed by human science, by human experience; for this form of determinism is definitely linked with accountability.

In order to have an accountable prediction task, we must be given a *model* of the system (as I indicated in section 15); that is to say, *an approximate description of its state.* This is clear if we consider that in order to solve a one-body problem or a two-body problem or, say, a three-body problem in which the interaction of two of the three bodies is negligible on a first approximation (because of their great distance and small masses), we shall not need so precise initial conditions as we need for solving, with the same degree of precision, a three-body problem with powerful interaction between *any* two of the three bodies. Yet if we have to be given the approximate initial state of the system before we can even begin to calculate the degree of approximation required by accountability, then the whole problem of accountability may become indeterminate, for some cases, if not insoluble. For the question arises: how good does the model have to be in order to allow us to calculate the approximation required by accountability? Since the goodness of the model is its degree of approximation or precision, we are threatened by an infinite regress; and the threat will be very serious for systems which are complex. But the complexity of the system can also be assessed only if an approximate model is at hand; a consideration which again indicates that we are threatened by an infinite regress.

No doubt, in many cases which are not too complex, it will be possible to proceed by the following method: we first obtain a model, which may be good or bad: we do not need to know. Then we try to calculate, according to the principle of accountability, the required precision of the initial conditions needed for completing our prediction task; and if we fail because the model first given was not good enough, we try to get a better model.

This method may often succeed; and if it does, we shall certainly say that accountability is satisfied. But what if we fail again, even with the better model? It is clear that we must, in advance, limit either the permissible number of demands for an improved model, or else the 'goodness', i.e., the degree of precision, which we may require of the model. But the task of calculating either of these may lead us merely to a problem of accountability of a higher order. And with this, we may be well on the way to an infinite regress. For there is no reason whatever to believe that the higher order problem is easier to solve than is the lower order problem, or that a less good model is needed for its solution than for the solution of the lower order problem. Nor is there any reason to believe that methods of approximation are always capable of improving results indefinitely.

These considerations are not offered as decisive, but rather as indications that, in connection with the problem of 'scientific' determinism, the problem of complexity may crucially affect the situation, and that the complexity of the real world is likely to destroy all arguments which maintain that determinism is based upon scientific experience or the success of our scientific theories.

Apart from these very general considerations, there are more specific ones, concerning accountability in both its weaker and its stronger senses (distinguished in section 3 above).

First, as to weak accountability, there is the fact that even if we are given exact initial conditions, we can only in special cases predict the future of a Newtonian system consisting of more than two bodies, and that there does not seem to be any hope for solving this task for more than three bodies unless the system belongs to those very special structures to which certain methods of approximation are applicable. With a system consisting, say, of eight, or of eighty, or of eight hundred approximately equal bodies, situated at approximately equal distances, we do not know how to deal. Since we have, at present, no method of calculating predictions for a complex system of this kind, we have, *a fortiori*, no method of finding out how precise any given set of initial conditions would have to be in order to solve a prediction task with a predetermined degree of precision.

As long as there is no serious prospect of solving the general *n*-body problem of Newtonian dynamics, there is no reason whatever to believe that Newtonian dynamics is accountable, even in the weaker sense of 'accountable'.

Moreover, if we proceed to examine the situation with respect to accountability in its stronger sense, we may find good reasons for believing that Newtonian dynamics is *not* accountable.

Let us consider an (approximately) isolated Newtonian

gravitating system, far away in empty space, consisting of a number of smallish bodies (of masses, say, between those of a few tons and those of a few dozens of tons). And let us consider how we could determine, by measurements, the initial conditions needed for predicting a system of this kind, and more especially the masses of the various bodies belonging to it. We cannot make use of a pendulum, or of a test body combined with a spring balance, because we cannot intrude into a system of this kind without disturbing it severely, and in an unpredictable way. (The disturbance is unpredictable because we know too little about the system which, owing to our intrusion, may become so unbalanced that some of its members may escape from it before we can measure them.) Thus we must assume that we can find the initial conditions of a system of this kind by *visually* observing it from outside, like a stellar system. We can assume that the system either provides its own sources of visible light or is illuminated by visible light from without; and we can assume that, by using visible light, we do not disturb the system. (This assumption is reasonable since the bodies of the system are macroscopic bodies, sufficiently heavy not to be appreciably disturbed by measurements with visible light—in contradistinction to the usual Heisenbergian view concerning atoms or sub-atomic particles.) We may even assume that we can measure velocities optically (with the help of Doppler's effect) rather than by measuring two positions and a time interval. (For example, we may observe three velocity vectors optically from three distant non-coplanar planets between which communication has been established.) In order to calculate the masses, or *at least* the mass-ratios, we have to use the inverse square law, and to measure (by radar, say), for the same instance of time, distances and accelerations.[1]

---

[1] See C. G. Pendse, *Phil. Mag.*, 7th series, **24**, pp. 1012 *ff.*, 1937; **27**, pp. 51 *ff.*, 1939; H and **29**, pp. 477 *ff.*, 1940. Pendse investigates the theory of the determination of mass-ratios by way of accelerations. In his comments on Pendse's work, V. V. Narlikar, *Phil. Mag.* **27**, pp. 33 *ff.*, rightly points out that in the presence of the inverse square law of force, mass-ratios can be obtained from the accelerations (a point not previously mentioned by Pendse and agreed upon by him in the last of these papers). Neither of these authors considers the inherent difficulty of measuring Newtonian non-constant accelerations at definite instants of time.

Now let us consider how we can measure *accelerations* optically. The only way is by measuring velocities and seeing how they change. But there is even a problem in measuring instantaneous velocities: the more precisely we wish to determine the velocities, the less precise will be the determination of the instant to which they belong. But even if (by way of concession to our opponents) we should be prepared to disregard this difficulty, it comes up again in a more severe form if we measure acceleration. For in order to do so, we must measure velocities in two instants of time which are separated by a finite, not too short interval of time; otherwise we would not be able to observe any appreciable difference, and consequently fail to measure the acceleration; yet if we take a not too short interval, then we cannot attribute the accelerations to any precise instant; and we obtain, in addition, merely average accelerations.

The mathematics of this may be simplified as follows. For light coming from a source, we have the general formula

$$(1) \qquad \Delta \nu \Delta t = 1$$

If we apply this to Doppler's effect which may be written

$$(2) \qquad v = \lambda_0 (\nu_0 - \nu_1)$$

then we find that we can determine ν_0 and therefore λ_0 as precisely as we like: they refer to light from a constant source which we may in principle observe as long as we like. Thus we may take ν_0 and λ_0 as exactly known. But the shift $\nu_0 - \nu_1$ cannot be measured more precisely than ν_1. Thus we obtain by combining (1) and (2)

$$(3) \qquad \Delta v \Delta t = \lambda_0$$

Since we have assumed that we operate with visible light (this assumption can be somewhat weakened, but there is a lower limit to λ_0 because too hard light would have too great penetrating power) there will be a lower limit to λ_0; and accordingly, we see from (3) that we cannot make both Δv and Δt independently as small as we like. However, (3) is only valid for constant velocities; for changing velocities, the situation concerning v is even worse than expressed by (3). For if v changes, as we must assume it does since we are interested in measuring acceleration,

53

there are two different sources, each tending to increase the size of Δv: first, the choice of a *small* Δt, i.e., of a small period of measurement (or of exposure of the photographic plate on which we record the shift), which increases Δv in accordance with (3) or (1); secondly, the choice of a *large* Δt, with the consequence that v and v_1 change during the period of measurement, so that v_1 becomes 'smeared', and consequently Δv large. There will be, accordingly (at best) an optimal value of Δt, depending upon the acceleration, such that Δt is large enough (from the point of view of formula (3)) and yet not too large to allow the acceleration to increase Δv. Corresponding to that optimal value of Δt, there will be a smallest value of Δv—one which we cannot decrease.

If we now try to determine the acceleration a, based upon a second measurement (of v_2 made at the time t_2) so that

$$(4) \qquad\qquad a \approx \frac{v_2 - v_1}{t_2 - t_1}$$

then we see at once that if the interval $t_2 - t_1$ is not considerably greater than Δt, we obtain a completely indeterminate value such as $a = 0/0$. Thus it becomes in principle impossible to determine a precisely for any short interval of time Δt; rather, we can only obtain an average value of a for a much longer period $t_2 - t_1$, where t_1 and t_2 are each determined merely with a limited precision Δt, and where even the *average* value of a is only imprecisely determined, owing to the irreducible imprecision of v_1 and v_2 ($v_2 - v_1$ has also to be much greater than Δv).

It is clear, from these considerations, that we cannot, with the help of visible light, measure in our Newtonian system as precisely as we like all the various accelerations at a certain instant (to be determined as precisely as we like). Consequently, we cannot determine the mass ratios of the bodies as precisely as we like. It does not seem, therefore, that even in all macroscopic classical systems measurements are possible which could give us the initial conditions as precisely as we like; and this leads at once to the conclusion that not all prediction tasks of classical physics can be carried out on the basis of measurements of initial conditions.

A fortiori this means, furthermore, that classical physics is not accountable, in the stronger sense of 'accountable'.

The similarity between the situation in classical physics described here and the principle of indeterminacy which, according to Heisenberg, holds for quantum theory, is too obvious to need further comment. (Heisenberg's indeterminacy formulae are, of course, the same as formula (1): they result simply from multiplying both sides of (1) by h or by $\hbar$.) The similarity is the result of applying, like Heisenberg, an operationalist analysis. But since, unlike Heisenberg, I am not an operationalist, I do not use these considerations to derive ontological consequences; rather, I wish only to point out difficulties inherent in the view that Newtonian mechanics differs from the quantum theory in being deterministic.

18. *The Past and the Future.*

The approximate character of all scientific knowledge—the net whose mesh we try to make finer and finer—furnishes what seems to me the philosophically most fundamental argument against 'scientific' determinism, and in favour of indeterminism. Secondary to it, but still important, is *the argument from the asymmetry between the past and the future.*

One cannot change the past—though attempts have been made to do the next thing to it (and a thing which, according to idealism or subjectivism or positivism would be the same): changing our knowledge of the past by perverting existing historical records. Since the past is nothing but what has happened, it is trivially true that *the past is completely determined by what has happened.* The determinist doctrine—according to which the future is also completely determined by what has happened—wantonly destroys a fundamental asymmetry in the structure of our experience;[1] and it is in striking conflict with common sense. All our

---

[1] The asymmetry I am alluding to entails, clearly, the *'arrow of time'*; but it entails more than the assertion that time has a direction (an 'arrow'). For this arrow has been found in the past and will be found in the future: its existence does not suffice to establish the fundamental difference between past and future

lives, all our activities, are occupied by attempts to affect the future. Clearly, we believe that what will happen in the future is largely determined by the past or the present, for all our present rational actions are attempts to influence, or to determine, the future. (This holds even for attempts to pervert the past.) But just as clearly, we do look upon the future as not yet completely fixed; in contrast to the past which is closed, as it were, the future is still open to influence; it is not yet completely determined.

I am far from asserting that, in matters of this kind, common sense and common attitudes are the ultimate arbiters: if there are good reasons, based upon arguments, and especially upon test-able scientific theories, for accepting a view in conflict with common sense, then I have no doubt what attitude to adopt. This, however, is not the case here. For there are even good

which I have in mind. As to the *arrow of time*, it is in my opinion a mistake to make the second law of thermodynamics responsible for its direction. Even a non-thermodynamic process, such as the propagation of a wave from a centre, is in fact irreversible. Suppose a film is taken of a large surface of water initially at rest into which a stone has been dropped: no physicist will mistake the end of the film strip for its beginning; for the creation of a contracting circular wave followed by a zone of undisturbed water approaching the center would be (causally considered) miraculous. If this is contested by saying that the allegedly miraculous phenomenon might have been caused by a multiplicity of oscillators arranged in a huge circle and working in unison ('coherently'), then I should answer that this arrangement would be miraculous unless steered or co-ordinated *from a centre,* e.g., by light signals; so that, in order to establish the physical and causal possibility of the inverted film, we should have to assume that it is *preceded by a process in which waves do not contract but spread,* as in the original film; a process which, if the film is again inverted, becomes in its turn miraculous, and thus creates an infinite regress. In other words, all causes (although not all forces) spread from centres (reminiscent of Huygens's principle); and the arrow of time is due, in the case considered, not to the equations but to the character of the initial conditions. See also A. Einstein, *Physikalische Zeitschrift* 10, 1909, p. 821; and my own letters, 'The Arrow of Time', *Nature* 177, 1956, p. 538; 'Irreversibility and Mechanics', *Nature* 178, 1956, pp. 381 *ff.*; and 'Irreversible Processes in Physical Theory', *Nature* 179, 1957, pp. 1296*ff.* [See also Popper's 'Irreversibility; or Entropy since 1905', *British Journal for the Philosophy of Science* 8, 1957, pp. 151–5; 'Erratum', *Ibid.* 8, 1957, p. 258; 'Irreversible Processes in Physical Theory', *Nature* 181, 1958, pp. 402–3; 'Time's Arrow and Entropy', *Nature* 207, 1965, pp. 233–4; 'Time's Arrow and Feeding on Negentropy', *Nature* 213, 1967, p. 320; 'Structural Information and the Arrow of Time', *Nature* 214, 1967, p. 322; 'Autobiography of Karl Popper', in P. A. Schilpp, ed.: *The Philosophy of Karl Popper*, Vol. I, pp. 124–129, and Vol. II, pp. 1140–44; and *Unended Quest*, pp. 156–162. Ed.]

scientific reasons, stemming from a *prima facie* deterministic theory—the special theory of relativity—which support the commonsense view of the 'openness' of the future.

19. *The Verdict of Special Relativity.*

If I am right in asserting an asymmetry between the past and the future—the closedness of the past, and the openness of the future—then this asymmetry ought to be represented in the structure of physical theory.

This demand is fully satisfied by Einstein's special theory of relativity.[1] In this theory there exists for every observer—or, as I prefer to say, for every local inertial system—an absolute past and an absolute future (which are separated by a whole region of possible contemporaneity). The (absolute) past of the system is the region formed by all spatio-temporal points from which physical influences (for example, light signals) can affect the system; its (absolute) future is the region formed by all points upon which a physical influence may be exerted by the system. In Minkowski's geometrical representation, this past and this future form the two cones (more precisely the two parts of a four-dimensional double cone); its apex A is 'the here-and-now'.

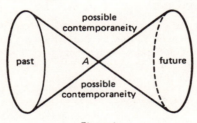

Figure 1

---

[1] Unfortunately, the position is otherwise as regards Einstein's general theory of relativity: here the asymmetry of the special theory becomes a local affair. But this fact is indirectly acknowledged by Einstein as a blemish to be removed (even *ad hoc,* if no better method is available). See *Albert Einstein, Philosopher-Scientist,* ed. P. A. Schilpp, 1949, esp. p. 687, i.e., Einstein's reply to Kurt Gödel. See also the next footnote. [See also *Unended Quest,* pp. 129–32 and notes 201 and 202. Ed.]

A cut through the cone looks like this—

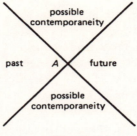

Figure 2

(I have arranged this diagram so that the time points from the left to the right, as is usual in diagrammatic presentations, although in diagrams of relativity it is more usual to let the time axis point upward.)

I shall not discuss this well-known diagram in detail. But I should point out that it fully satisfies the demand of the asymmetry between future and past. In physical terms, this asymmetry is established by the fact that from any place in the 'past', a physical causal chain (for example, a light signal) can reach any place in the 'future'; but from no place in the future can such an effect be exerted on any place in the past.[2]

---

[2] On this point, the general theory differs from the special one, as Gödel has shown (*cp.* the foregoing footnote). No doubt the solutions mentioned by Gödel do not agree with the ideas underlying the general theory, and ought to be excluded, as Einstein has suggested (*op. cit.*, p. 688). But an *ad hoc* solution would not be satisfactory. As long as the exclusion is not obtained from a modification of the equations themselves, the following *'principle of the unbroken connection of world-lines'* may be relied upon to achieve it. It is a principle which seems to me implicit in the very idea of local time as well as in the principle that special relativity must hold locally within the general theory. In operational terms, my principle may be formulated as follows. *Any 'observer' (local material system) can begin, at any instant, a record (causal trace); make successive entries into that record; and arrange for the preservation of the record for any desired finite period of time.* (By 'can' the following is meant: the theoretical possibility of any world-line, to be considered as consistent with the laws of nature, must not entail the impossibility of the operations described in the above principle.) If this principle is adopted, then the existence of an 'observer' (a material system) whose world-line is closed in time leads to a

But as a consequence of this, the future becomes *'open'* to us in the sense that it cannot be fully predicted *by us*, while the past is 'closed'; that is to say, the asymmetry is of the kind which I have tried to establish.

In order to see this, let us assume that we are at the apex *A* and wish to make a complete prediction about the state of affairs in our system when it will have arrived at the spatio-temporal point *B*.

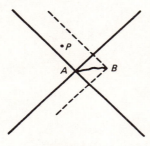

Figure 3

It is well known[3] that we cannot do this: as Fig. 3 shows, there are points such as *P*, which belong to the past of *B* but not to that of *A;* which means that from *P*, effects may reach *B;* but it is impossible for us, at *A*, to know anything about the conditions at *P*, since no effect from *P* can reach us in *A*: *P* is outside the past-cone of *A*; but the past-cone of *A* is the only region about which we can have knowledge.

contradiction; for, as can easily be shown, the existence of a closed world-line (which, for the sake of consistency, must be infinitely and absolutely repetitive) would entail the periodic destruction of every single record (causal trace), since otherwise the trace (or track) would not be fully repetitive but would constantly enrich itself upon every renewal of the closed journey. The adoption of my principle would make the 'way in which matter and its motion are arranged in the world' (*op.cit.*, p. 562) depend upon its time structure (which my principle helps to characterize) rather than the other way round. The same result may be obtained—still less *ad hoc*—by adopting a *'principle of indeterminism'*: this too would automatically exclude all cosmological solutions permitting closed world-lines.

[3] *Cf.* Hermann Weyl, *Philosophy of Mathematics and Natural Science*, Princeton, 1949, pp. 210; 102.

I now want to show that, in consequence of this asymmetry between past and future, special relativity is no longer *prima facie* deterministic in the full sense described above. I shall do this by showing that there is no longer a Laplacean demon in special relativity.

Take again the situation in Fig. 3; *A* is our present, and *B* is a spatio-temporal point about which a prediction is to be made. Human scientists cannot make it; but we assume that there is a Laplacean demon—one who is capable of obtaining *all* the initial conditions for a sufficiently big (but limited) region of space at a certain instant of time, i.e., for a certain region which may be said to be 'simultaneous' in the sense of special relativity. In our Fig. 4, this region is represented by the line segment *C*.

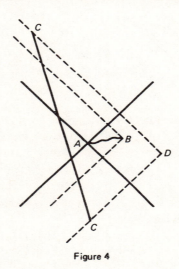

Figure 4

It is clear that for the purpose of predicting the state of affairs at *B*, the line *C* must reach *at least* up to the dotted lines indicating the past of *B;* but we may assume that it goes beyond it. Thus *C* represents the region about which the demon has received complete information. Now given this region, the theory allows us to find a spatio-temporal position *D* which, from the point of view of the theory, is the *earliest* spatio-temporal position at which the demon may be located when receiving the information. And D will be so located that B belongs to the past of D. This means that the demon, when calculating the state of affairs at B, was making a retrodiction rather than a prediction—in terms of special relativity. Or in other words: *if we try to introduce the Laplacean demon into special relativity, we find that we can calculate, from the demon's region of information, a lower bound for the demon's spatio-temporal position D; and we further find that the demon calculated only an event within his own past.*

If the line C is made infinitely long in both directions—which turns our limited demon into an unlimited demon—then we find that the demon can indeed calculate *any* event. But this is so because he is, in terms of the theory, situated in the infinite future, so that *any* event belongs to his past.

Thus the demon of special relativity is no longer that of Laplace; for this demon, as opposed to Laplace's, cannot predict; he can only retrodict.

To sum up, special relativity automatically turns every event about which we—or a demon—can have some definite information into an event which belongs to our past—or to the past of the demon. Thus it may be said that, according to special relativity, the past is that region which can, in principle, be known; and the future is that region which, although influenced by the present, is always 'open': it is not only unknown, but in principle not fully knowable, since by becoming completely known, even to a demon, it would become part of the demon's past. Special relativity, in spite of its *prima facie* determinist character, cannot therefore be used to support 'scientific' determinism, for two reasons. (1) The predictions demanded by 'scientific' determinism must be interpreted, from the point of view of special relativity itself, as *retrodictions*. (2) Being retrodictions, they appear, from the point of view of special relativity, to be computed in the future of the predicted system. Thus they cannot be said to be computed within that system: they do not satisfy the principle of *predictability from within*.

The existence of the theory of special relativity refutes, in this way, the usual assumption that it would be permissible to derive

61

the truth of 'scientific' determinism from the truth of a *prima facie* deterministic theory.

20. *Historical Prediction and the Growth of Knowledge.*

> Do not, therefore, expect any prophecy from me: had I known what one will discover tomorrow, I would have published it long ago, to secure priority.
>
> HENRI POINCARÉ

Apart from criticizing determinism, I have discussed so far two positive arguments in favour of indeterminism: that from the approximate character of scientific knowledge and that from the asymmetry of the past and the future.

I now come to a third argument, less fundamental perhaps than either of these two, but still very important, especially since it will help to construct a formal refutation of 'scientific' determinism (as will be seen in section 23). I shall first state the argument in human terms. Surprisingly enough, it can be completely restated—and in fact, stated more precisely—in purely physical terms.

The core of the argument is the consideration that there are certain things about ourselves which we cannot ourselves predict by scientific methods; more especially, *we cannot predict, scientifically, results which we shall obtain in the course of the growth of our own knowledge.* Others who are wiser than we may be able to predict the growth of *our* knowledge, just as we may be able under certain circumstances to predict the growth of a child's knowledge; *but they too will not be able to predict or anticipate today what they themselves will know only tomorrow.*

This formulation indicates that there may be a real contradiction involved in the idea of predicting today what we shall know only tomorrow; and so there is. But it is not easy to make sure that this contradiction is not due merely to our formulation, and that it actually prevents the possibility of complete self-prediction. That it does so will be shown in the next two sections.

Here I wish to point out some of the consequences of the statement that *there cannot be a scientist able to predict all the results of all his own predictions*.

One of these consequences is that he will not be able to predict some of his own future states; and, further, not all the states of his own 'neighbourhood', i.e., of the part of his environment which he appreciably influences. For if he does not know what he will know tomorrow, he cannot know how he will act tomorrow upon his environment. Thus the state of his neighbourhood will not be completely predictable by himself *from within*, although it may be predictable *from without*, by observers who can predict his actions, provided they neither interfere appreciably with him, nor with his neighbourhood.

It follows that no physical system can be completely predicted from within (and that the predictability of such systems as the solar system should be described, in the terminology of section 11, as predictability from without).

The argument can be used to *refute the doctrine of historicism*—the doctrine that the task of the social sciences is to predict the course of human history. For we may argue as follows:

(1) If complete self-prediction can be shown to be impossible, whatever the complexity of the predictor, then this must also hold for any 'society' of interacting predictors; consequently, no 'society' of interacting predictors can predict its own future states of knowledge.

(2) The course of human history is strongly influenced by the growth of human knowledge. (The truth of this premise must be admitted even by those who, like the Marxists, see in our ideas, including our scientific ideas, merely the by-products of material developments of one kind or another.)

(3) We cannot, therefore, predict the future course of human history; not, at any rate, those of its aspects which are strongly influenced by the growth of our knowledge.

This argument does not, of course, deny the possibility of every social prediction; on the contrary, it is perfectly compatible with the possibility of testing social theories—for example, economic theories (but not 'historical theories')—by deriving from them predictions asserting that certain developments will take place under certain conditions, and by testing these predictions.[1]

21. *Predicting the Growth of Theoretical Knowledge.*

Let us consider more closely what a prediction of the growth of scientific knowledge may involve. It may involve our ability to predict now that at some future date we shall either (a) *accept* (tentatively, of course) *as well-tested certain theories* not accepted at present and perhaps unknown at present; or (b) derive certain now unknown *explanations or predictions* from theories now accepted or later accepted, in conjunction with initial conditions (which may be as yet unknown).

In the present section I shall deal with predictions of the growth of theoretical knowledge, i.e., with problem (a). Here the important question is whether we might be able to predict the *acceptance of a previously not accepted theory on the basis of new tests.* Of lesser importance is a preliminary question: whether we might be able to predict *the content of an as yet unknown theory*—the new idea which will occur to somebody, or which will be propounded by somebody.

The reason why I say that this is of lesser importance is that often when a theory is new, in the sense that it is newly accepted, it turns out that it is not quite as new as it looks. It may even have been propounded long ago and forgotten because there was no evidence in favour of it, or no problem yet for which it was needed, or which it was able to solve. This shows that what is important, *if we are mainly interested in the growth of 'accepted' knowledge* as opposed to the growth of new ideas, is the tentative

[1] All these problems are discussed, in some detail, in my book *The Poverty of Historicism*, 1957; first published in *Economica*, 1944–5, and in my paper 'Prediction and Prophecy and their Significance for Social Theory', now reprinted in *Conjectures and Refutations*, Chapter 16. In *The Poverty of Historicism*, I only tried to show that historicism is a poor method; I did not try to refute it. The refutation given here in the text is implicit in my articles on Indeterminism, quoted above; it is explicitly stated in my Preface to the French edition (Paris, 1956) of the *Poverty*, and to the English book-edition (1957).

acceptance of a theory, on the basis of new problems, or new evidence.

Now let us first consider the preliminary question of the growth of our new theoretical ideas. A psychologist or, if you like, a physiologist may well predict the theories or expectations which a child (or an animal), under the influence of certain environmental stimuli, may form and, after certain tests, accept: the burnt child (or cat) dreads the fire. If our psychological (or physiological or physical or economic . . .) knowledge is very good we might imagine that we are able to apply a similar method to ourselves, and predict today the theories which will *for the first time* occur to us in, say, one month, under the influence of certain environmental stimuli which will begin to act upon us (according to our knowledge of our physical or economic environment) in, say, three weeks' time.

Now there is something absurd in this way of putting the matter. For, if we knew today, it may be argued, what theories will occur to us for the first time a month ahead, then the theory would, of course, occur to us today, in some sense or other, and not in one month; consequently, we did not foresee anything that may be described as the future growth of knowledge.

Against this argument, which I consider valid, the following objection may be raised. We may predict today that an idea will occur to somebody in a month's time, and that it will only then become known and influential; and today's prediction is to be kept secret. But this objection entails that we predicted the system *from without* rather than from within; for we took measures (secrecy) not to influence it. Thus it was not a prediction about 'ourselves'. Moreover, even assuming that we do ourselves belong to the system about which we have made a prediction, we could only *decide* to keep our results secret; and we must not naïvely assume that we can predict, scientifically, that we shall carry out our decisions—especially if circumstances change, owing to an unexpected growth of our knowledge. The assumption that we can predict such things of ourselves would amount to begging the question at issue—whether self-prediction is possible.

Another objection looks different, but in the end amounts to the same. It is that we may predict the growth of knowledge without *understanding* what we predict. We may predict, say, the black shapes which a writer is to write on white paper, and their repercussions upon history, without understanding all, or even anything, that he intends to convey. In this case it cannot be said that we have anticipated the theories by predicting them.

The reply is, again, that if we can predict, i.e., describe these shapes, we, or anybody aware of our predictions, can write them down now; and if their genesis is to influence history in the future, there is no reason why it should not do so now. Admittedly, they may have different effects in different circumstances; but this does not concern us here. All that concerns us at the moment is that it seems pretty pointless to say that we can predict the genesis of new ideas from within the system.[1]

I come now to the more important question of the prediction of the *acceptance* of a theory under the influence of new evidence.

In order not to get into the same trouble as before, we should have to assume that the new evidence in question is not available to us now. Otherwise, our prediction would amount to pointing out that there is now evidence in favour of a not yet accepted theory, and that the theory ought, by rights, to be accepted now. In other words, the prediction would again not be of the future growth of knowledge, but it would be, rather, a statement about what we know now.

It would be necessary, therefore, to assume that we can predict—on the basis of our present knowledge, i.e., of now accepted theories—events not yet observed which, when ob-

---

[1] My argument uses the fact that every prediction of a system from within may influence the system; for example, the prediction of an otherwise new idea changes its character of newness. I have used the term 'Oedipus-effect' as a name for the influence, upon the predicted event, of a theory, or an expectation, or a prediction, or even information used to obtain a prediction: it will be remembered that it was partly the influence of the oracle's prediction which brought about the predicted event. *Cp.* my papers on 'Indeterminism', *op. cit.*, pp. 188 f.; *The Poverty of Historicism*, section 5; and 'Philosophy of Science: A Personal Report' in *British Philosophy in the Mid-Century*, 1957, the second footnote. [This last essay is reprinted as 'Science: Conjectures and Refutations' in *Conjectures and Refutations*, pp. 33–65. Ed.]

served, will furnish evidence in support of some not yet accepted theory, and thus lead to its acceptance.

But this is impossible. Evidence whose occurrence can be predicted on the basis of our present knowledge cannot be evidence which would justify the acceptance of a new theory. For evidence which can be predicted with the help of present knowledge would either not be new in kind, or if new, would amount to a test confirming our present theories (rather than inducing us to accept a new theory). The kind of evidence which would justify the acceptance of a new theory is evidence which can be predicted with the help of the new theory but *not* with the help of our present knowledge; in other words, it must have the character of *crucial* evidence.

To me this argument is not quite without interest. In spite of a certain triviality—for it says hardly more than that every theory entails its own truth,[2] and therefore cannot predict a situation which involves its rejection—it suffices for a refutation of the influential doctrine of historicism; for it shows that we cannot, by scientific procedures, predict the growth of our theoretical knowledge. (We could, *at best,* predict, at any time, that our knowledge is not growing any longer—that our present theories are all true, and complete.)

All this still leaves an important question open. What if we *assume* that the growth of our theoretical knowledge has come to an end, and that our theories are true as well as complete? This would still allow a certain kind of growth; for there would still be the endless task of applying our theories to ever new and ever different initial conditions. Thus the question arises: if we were Laplacean demons in the sense that we were to know all universal laws, and also all relevant initial conditions applying to ourselves, could we then predict our own future predictions?

---

[2] I am alluding to Tarski's work on the concept of truth according to which every statement (or more precisely, its translation into a semantic metalanguage) is equivalent to the metalinguistic assertion that it is true.

22. *The Impossibility of Self-Prediction.*

We thus come to the last, most decisive, and most abstruse of the questions connected with the predictability of the growth of our knowledge. It is the following:

Assuming we are furnished with perfect theoretical knowledge and present or past initial conditions, could we then predict, by *deductive methods,* our own future states for any given instant of time, and more especially, our own future predictions?

I shall of course only attempt to prove the impossibility of *scientific* self-prediction, i.e., of *deducing* a self-prediction from universal theories (assumed to be true), in conjunction with true initial information about one's own initial state. For non-scientific kinds of self-prediction may well be successful. There is, for example, self-prediction based upon decisions to act in a certain way. Thus I may predict today that I shall give two lectures tomorrow. Or I may predict today that I shall write tomorrow a letter to my friend Fred which will begin with the prediction: 'You will be surprised to hear that . . .'. Self-predictions of this kind are not of the scientific type; they are not based upon well-tested universal theories in conjunction with initial conditions, but upon a process of *'making up one's mind'*. Nor can they be replaced by scientific predictions based upon the law, 'whenever I make up my mind to write a letter on the next day, I always carry out my decision', in conjunction with the initial condition, 'I have just made up my mind to write a letter to Fred tomorrow'; if only because I am not a closed system, which means that the initial conditions of the system described are incomplete: I may receive a cable tonight informing me that Fred will arrive tomorrow, or that other new circumstances relevant to my decision have arisen.

Now once we assume that the scientific theories and the initial conditions are given, and also the prediction task, the derivation of the prediction becomes a problem of mere calculation, which in principle can be carried out by *a predicting or a calculating machine*—a 'calculator' or a 'predictor', as it may be called. This makes it possible to present my proof in the form of a proof that *no calculator or predictor can deductively predict the results of its own calculations or predictions.*

The method of couching our problem in terms of calculating machines has several minor advantages. First, in doing so I make a concession to my deterministic adversaries (whether they are 'materialists' or 'physicalists' or 'cyberneticists'); which may persuade them in their turn to consider my arguments more sympathetically. Secondly, it allows me to give a refutation of determinism without assuming the existence of *minds*. It allows me, therefore, to give a refutation which is more general than one which would have to rely upon the peculiarities of human predictors. Thirdly, everything said about the machines will hold, with trivial changes, for human predictors also. A fourth reason is that the method imposes a certain discipline upon those who use it. It has only one disadvantage as far as I can see: that I may be mistaken for one of those who believe that men are machines, although I believe nothing of the kind.[1]

The main advantage, however, of discussing our problem in terms of the capabilities of predicting machines is this. We can imagine a comparatively simple machine which represents a kind of simplified model of a *prima facie* deterministic theory, and which is definitely *predictable from without*. (It may even be a machine capable of discrete states only, so that all questions connected with the problem of the limited precision of initial

---

[1] See also the last section of the present chapter, partly based upon my paper on 'Indeterminism', quoted above, especially upon pp. 193–5 of the second part. I may mention here that I believe that, in principle, machines can be built which are capable of performing *any specified task which human beings can perform*. The emphasis is here upon the words 'any specified': for a specification can be used, in principle, for constructing a machine. For this reason, I am not prepared to accept the mechanist's challenge, '*specify precisely* a test which only a human being can pass and which it is in principle impossible for a machine to pass!' If we *specify precisely* the tests to be carried out in order to find out whether we are confronted by a man or a machine, we must face the possibility that a machine will be built *to these specifications*, and so pass the specified test. This, however, does not mean that, if confronted with a particular man-like machine, we should have the slightest difficulty in finding plenty of tests which the machine would fail to pass, especially if we had its specification (or even if we merely proceeded by the method of trial and error), although few human beings would fail them. See also my paper 'Language and the Body-Mind Problem', *Proceedings of the XIth International Congress of Philosophy*, 1953, vol. vii, pp. 101 *ff*. [The latter is reprinted in *Conjectures and Refutations*, pp. 293–8. See also *The Self and Its Brain*, p. 208. Ed.]

conditions may be ignored.) At the same time, the machine may be considered *as a perfect incarnation, a perfect physical embodiment, of Laplace's demon.*

In order to achieve this, we shall take the predictor to be a machine of the following kind.

Into the predictor have been built (a) all true universal laws of physics, and (b) all relevant calculation methods of mathematics and logic.

The predictor is so constructed that if, and only if, it is in a certain state—its 'zero state'—it may be stimulated by a *prediction task.* It then shuts itself off from further stimuli and proceeds to work until it has completed its task by working out a *reply*, i.e., a prediction.

The prediction *task* may be taken to consist of the description of some system's initial state, or state at 'zero time', $t_0 = 0$; it must refer, furthermore, to an instant of time, t_1 say, which is that instant of time for which the state of the system is to be predicted. The prediction will constitute the predictor's *reply*. Of course, what we are mainly interested in is this reply: it will represent the *addition to knowledge* which the predictor is to achieve, and therefore the 'growth of its knowledge'.

As a quite inessential assumption (but useful in so far as it simplifies certain matters), we may add that, upon having issued its reply, the predictor will return to its zero state.

In order to make our considerations more concrete, we can imagine that the prediction task is supplied to the machine in the form of a tape (the *'task tape'*) into which holes are punched, forming a coded message, in a code similar to Morse. The reply is issued in the form of a similar tape, the *'reply tape'*. Upon completion of its task, the machine may be assumed to consist of two main parts, that is to say (a) the machine itself (in a narrower sense) which may be in its zero state, and (b) the issued reply tape.

The following two assumptions, (A1) and (A2), about the predictor are essential.

(A1) Provided the task supplied to the machine was sufficiently explicit (i.e., sufficient for Laplace's demon to arrive at a prediction) the predictor will always arrive at a correct reply.

This assumption is intended to ensure that the predictor is sufficiently powerful. The next assumption is intended to ensure that it is not disembodied, but a physical machine.

(A2) The predictor *takes time* to carry out its various operations. In particular, there will be a lapse of time between the instant of time in which the predictor is stimulated by the prediction task (insertion of the task tape) and the instant of time in which the predictor begins to write (punch) its reply. Furthermore, the writing (punching) of the reply also takes some time.

This assumption excludes, for example, machines which are not only endowed with perfect *theoretical* knowledge but which are omniscient, or semi-omniscient, in the sense that some replies are already built into them, and therefore need not be computed. We may say that, from our point of view, machines so endowed would be *ad hoc*, even if they were not only able to answer one or two questions in this way but very many.

From these assumptions, (A1) and (A2), it can be proved easily that in the case of a self-prediction task, the reply can only be complete *after* the event predicted, or at best at the same time. This is sufficient to establish our point—that the predictor cannot predict the *future* growth of its own knowledge.

However, if we strengthen our assumptions a little, we can prove more; we can then prove that the predictor will fail altogether in its task. The additional two assumptions needed are as follows:

(A3) Of any two replies issued by the predictor, the longer reply will take up more time than the shorter one.

The fourth assumption is the one which is decisive for our proof that the predictor will fail, and it will have to be discussed at some length. It is the following:

(A4) All replies given by the machine describe the state of some physical system explicitly in one and the same standard code or language; or, in other words, we exclude any special replies which use a special kind of code or language.

Two different considerations lead to this assumption. First, we must ensure that the reply given by the machine is explicit, because *in this lies the whole purpose of the machine*. For in an implicit sense, the machine 'knows' the reply the moment it is supplied with the initial conditions of the system under investigation. This is so because we have assumed that the reply is entailed by the laws built into the machine, in conjunction with these initial conditions; and moreover—see (A1)—that the machine is capable of correctly responding to this information. Thus all that is left to be done by the machine is *to make the implied prediction explicit*. Thus (A4) only expresses more definitely that the machine is able to fulfil its task.

As indicated, (A2) has the function of excluding, for example, *ad hoc* predictions, that is to say, trivial pseudo-computing machines. The need for this exclusion becomes even more clear when we consider the second consideration by which we may support (A4). It is the following:

If we wish our predictor to operate like a 'scientific' machine, i.e., one which deduces its replies from laws and initial conditions, then clearly we must exclude certain *ad hoc arrangements for self-prediction*. For example, we can interpret any physical system which changes periodically as a self-predicting system; thus we may interpret the night as a prediction of the coming day, or of the next night, etc. As a limiting case, we may even interpret an unchanging system as a self-predicting one. For example, a 'machine' consisting of an empty sheet of paper may, by agreement, be interpreted as containing a predictive message on the following lines: 'As long as I am not interfered with, my physical state will be, at any future time *t,* that of an empty sheet of paper.'[2] Such examples serve to remind us that we are interested only in 'scientific' machines or *deductive* predictors which are not designed *ad hoc* for self-prediction but are capable of deductively predicting at least a large class of different physical systems (and among them, if possible, systems very similar to themselves). We must not forget that we are interested in the problem of self-prediction mainly *because fundamentally we are interested in the*

[2] I owe the idea of this 'machine' to a personal communication received about 1950 from the late Dr A. M. Turing.

problem whether a predictor can predict changes in those parts of its own environment with which it strongly interacts. But this implies that we are only interested in predictors of very general predicting abilities which go far beyond any *ad hoc* methods of self-prediction of the kind described.

Now the use of such *ad hoc predictors* was implicitly excluded by our assumption (A2); what was not excluded by (A2), however, is the adoption of *ad hoc methods of interpretation,* in connection with predictors which satisfy (A2). For example, we may agree that an otherwise quite 'normal' predictor—i.e., one answering (A1) and (A2)—is, if in its zero state, to be interpreted as expressing the message: 'I am a physical system in such-and-such a state (here we should have to insert the physical description of this predictor in its zero state) and I shall be at all times in this state unless I am being stimulated by a task.' This particular interpretation may perhaps be said to be excluded by (A2); but there may be similar ones (for example, the periodic systems mentioned above) which are not so excluded.

In order to exclude all such *ad hoc* methods, we shall have to demand that when it comes to a self-prediction task, the predictor shall still proceed by *essentially the same methods* which it applies to all other tasks. In the form just given, the demand is a little too vague (as the words 'essentially' and 'methods' indicate); at the same time, it is also a little too sweeping; at any rate, it seems stronger than necessary. For it turns out that all we need is just the assumption (A4) which confines our demand to the *reply,* and to the language in which it is formulated.[3]

Assumption (A4) excludes the possibility of adopting the convention (for example) that an otherwise normal predictor in its nth state is to be interpreted as describing itself, and as predicting that it will move from this state into the $n + 1$st state

---

[3] It need not be assumed that *all tasks* are also to be explicitly formulated in one language. We may assume that the task, with the initial conditions, is somehow given to the machine; and we need not ask how. (See also the last footnote to this section.)

(which, in fact, it is about to move into, and which admittedly can always be calculated from the previous state).

This is all we assume about the prediction machine.

We now consider two structurally identical predictors. Predictor No. 1 is called 'Tell', because it is to foretell the state of No. 2; predictor No. 2 is called 'Told', because it is to be foretold by Tell. (Tell aims at Told, as it were.)

We assume that the initial conditions supplied to Tell as part of its prediction task describes the state of Told at zero hours ($t_0 = 0$), and that Tell's task is to predict the state of Told at 1 o'clock ($t_1 = 1$). The description of Told's initial state, as supplied to Tell, will have to include a description of the prediction task (the task tape) by which Told is to be stimulated at zero hours. So Tell is now trying to compute the state of Told at the instant of time $t_1 = 1$ o'clock, or what amounts to the same, the state of Told after the lapse of a period of time of 1 hour's length.

According to our assumption (A1), Tell will always succeed in this task of predicting Told.

We now assume that it so happens that the task given to Tell coincides precisely with the task to be given to Told at zero hours; in other words, Tell's task specifies that Told will be stimulated, at zero hours, to predict a third predictor. (This assumption is made in order that we may later interpret Tell's task as a self-prediction task.) We may formulate this as our assumption (B).

(B) Upon being stimulated by its prediction task, Tell will be in precisely the same state as Told will be upon being stimulated, at zero hours, by its prediction task. (There are serious reasons for doubting that we can ever succeed in supplying Tell with a prediction task informing Tell that Told is in a certain state S, if S is to coincide with Tell's own state upon being so informed.[4] But as a concession to my opponents, I here assume that we have succeeded in supplying Told with a task of this kind.)

Let us first assume that the time of 1 hour which we have chosen is so small that at 1 o'clock, Told will not yet have started

[4] *Cp.* the last footnote to this section.

74

punching its reply tape. (In this case, clearly, no growth of knowledge has taken place.) We can easily prove the following theorem (T1):

(T1) Under the conditions stated, the period of time taken by Tell to complete its task was longer than 1 hour.

The proof is trivial. Since Tell has completed its task, its reply has been completely punched. But after the lapse of 1 hour, it cannot even have started punching since Tell must run through the same states as Told, and in equal periods of time; and according to our assumptions, Told has not yet started work on its tape at 1 o'clock.

Next let us assume that we choose 2 o'clock instead of 1 o'clock as the time for which Tell is to predict the state of Told, and that Told has started punching its tape at 2 o'clock, without however completing it. For obvious reasons we get in this case the theorem (T2):

(T2) Under the conditions stated, the period of time taken by Tell to complete its task was longer than 2 hours.

The proof is analogous to the previous one.

Now let us finally assume that we chose 3 o'clock as the time for which Told's state is to be predicted, a period of time which is just long enough for Told to complete its prediction task. We obtain the theorem (T3):

(T3) Under the conditions stated, the time taken by Tell to complete its task was exactly equal to 3 hours.

This follows again from the fact that Tell and Told are identical machines; and it is sufficient to show that Tell cannot predict its own future growth of knowledge; for its completed reply would come too late to be a prediction since it can arrive, at best, only *together with the event predicted*.

I think that this result is reasonable and convincing, and that our three theorems establish all that is needed for our purpose: the prediction will in all cases come too late to be considered as a prediction of the *future growth of knowledge* of the machine.

This result has been derived without the use of either (A3) or (A4). This means that it is valid even if we introduce *ad hoc* some special symbolism (but it must be one which consumes *time* if it is used) which makes self-reference possible, and thus makes it possible for a description to describe itself.[5] (It is clear that this is the only case in which the self-calculation of its complete reply can possibly be completed by the machine, although too late to succeed as a self-prediction.)

But if we now decide to use (A3) and (A4), then it can be shown, I think, that self-calculation becomes altogether impossible: not only will it come late, but it will fail altogether.

This can be shown quite easily if we introduce a very simple and convincing further assumption—in fact, an auxiliary theorem or lemma. This lemma asserts that the description, in standard language (with the help of, say, a punched tape), of the physical state of a second description in standard language (of a second punched tape) can never be shorter than that second description (the second punched tape). This lemma seems to be true in view of the fact that we have to describe at least every symbol of the second description (the position of every hole in the tape), and that every such description will need, at the very least, one symbol.[6]

But if this lemma is granted, then we obtain the following theorem (T4) which contradicts theorem (T3) and therefore shows that the system of our assumptions must be inconsistent.

(T4) Under the conditions of theorem (T3) the time taken by Tell to complete its task was longer than three hours.

The proof is again quite simple, if the lemma is granted. Since Tell has to predict Told's state at 3 o'clock, it has to describe (a) the state of Told apart from its tape (it happens to be Told's 'zero state'), and (b) the state of Told's tape. But according to the lemma, Tell's description of (b) alone will be at least as long as the tape to be described. Therefore Tell's description of (a) and (b) together must be longer. In view of (A3) this establishes the theorem.

Now since (T3) and (T4) contradict each other, the set of our assumptions must be inconsistent. This means that, provided

---

[5] *Cp.* my paper on 'Indeterminism', etc., pp. 176 *ff.*
[6] This lemma was formulated in my paper on 'Indeterminism', etc., p. 177.

(A2), (A3), (A4), and the lemma, are all satisfied, either (A1) or (B) must be false. But this means, further, that *the predictor will fail to predict its own future state*, either because it cannot complete its computation, which means that (A1) fails; or because it could not be supplied with the required task, that is to say, with a description of its own state upon being supplied with this description.[7]

This result depends, of course, upon the lemma, and upon (A3) and (A4). But even without the lemma, and without (A3) and (A4), I have shown that a predictor cannot predict the result of its own future predictions—at least not before the 'predicted' event has actually taken place.

Thus we cannot predict the future growth of our own knowledge.

23. *The Refutation of 'Scientific' Determinism.*

We have proved that self-prediction is impossible, even if it should be possible to construct a predictor incorporating the powers of a Laplacean demon, and moving on the simplest mechanical principles—that is to say, a predictor which represents a physical system whose deterministic character is accepted without question.

Thus our proof cannot, admittedly, be used to refute deter-

---

[7] In my earlier paper on 'Indeterminism', quoted above, I myself raised (on p. 177) an objection against an argument which is similar to the second of the two proofs just sketched. This objection has no force against my present proof, however, in view of the arguments now advanced in support of assumption (A4). On the other hand, an analogous objection may be raised against the argument on p. 189 of my old paper, expounding the difficulty of supplying the machine with a task-tape describing this tape itself: we might supply the predictor (as against my old argument) with a self-describing tape (described on p. 177 of my old paper), provided the machine is fitted with an inbuilt 'dictionary', or a 'translation machine'. (I believe, however, that this would only shift the regress from the task-tape into the machine itself.) But although I believe that it could be proved, from a set of reasonable assumptions, that it is impossible to satisfy (B), i.e., to supply the predictor with a task-tape giving its own initial state in the instant of just having been supplied with the tape, I have decided to leave it open here whether it is (B) that fails or (A1).

minism. But it can be used to refute 'scientific' determinism, and with it any claim to base deterministic views upon any results of science, or upon the fact that science is successful.

For if self-prediction is impossible, then clearly a predictor cannot predict the effects of its own movements upon its own close environment, i.e., that part of its environment which it influences appreciably. And this means, further, that *prediction from within* cannot be carried out with any degree of precision which may be chosen, but only in so far as the interaction between the predictor and its environment may be neglected.

This result is supported by the success of science: we apply the method of scientific prediction only to systems which are not at all, or only slightly, affected by the prediction process. On the other hand, 'scientific' determinism requires that in principle we should be able to predict, from within, everything in our world with any degree of precision we choose; and since we ourselves are in our world, this doctrine is refuted by the impossibility of arbitrarily exact predictions from within, which is a consequence of the impossibility of self-prediction.

This result cannot be shaken by any attempt to operate with more than one predictor, provided all these predictors are *within the system in question:* a predictor other than our No. 1 may predict No. 1's difficulties; its states; and its influence upon the rest of the system; but it will not be able to predict its own influence (for example, upon No. 1). Moreover, a 'society' of interacting predictors[1] can always be considered, formally, as *one* complex predictor; and our result holds for predictors of any degree of complexity.

---

[1] The influence of the issued 'knowledge' (the reply) of a predictor upon another predictor (or any machine acting upon information) may be made as strong as we like: small differences in the reply tape—for example, the issuing of a reply tape issued by one machine to another containing one punched hole more or less—may make any difference we choose to the response of that other machine. As a consequence, a 'society' of predictors mutually influencing each other and attempting to predict each other may be highly unstable, and the individual predictors may lose their efficiency if they belong to a 'society' of this kind. Similar questions are dealt with in section 7 of my paper on 'Indeterminism', quoted above.

Since its refutation proceeds in effect by the use of logic alone, 'scientific' determinism turns out to be a self-contradictory doctrine. Thus nothing can support *scientific* determinism; and no appeal to a *prima facie* deterministic science, however complete, can support *any other form* of determinism. Kant's worries were therefore unnecessary; and no philosopher need worry about difficulties for his ethical convictions arising from a determinism based on the success of science (whether empirical or *a priori*).

Our refutation of 'scientific' determinism may seem to leave room for replacing 'scientific' determinism by a third version, untouched by our criticism. (I call it a third version in view of the two versions discussed in section 12.) This third version could be put in this way: every physical system is predictable in the sense that *at least after the event to be predicted has occurred,* we can see that the event was determined by the state of the system, in the sense that a sufficiently full description of the system (together with natural laws) *logically entails* the prediction. The fact that this prediction cannot always be calculated in advance does not affect the logical situation—as may be seen from the fact that we assumed, in our proof, a deterministic system. And it may be said, therefore, that my proof does not achieve its purpose.[2]

My reply to this criticism is that it misses my point. I do not wish to refute determinism which, I think, is irrefutable; I wish to refute what I have called 'scientific' determinism. It is perfectly true that, in doing so, I have not refuted the third version mentioned here. But I have refuted those who refer to *the actual success of scientific predictions* and who assert that this success justifies the assumption that we can, in principle, improve our predictions so as to make them as precise as we like. In other words, I wish to refute not only 'scientific' determinism, but also those who say that determinism (rather than 'scientific' deter-

---

[2] An argument that is very similar to the one given here has been advanced by W. B. Gallie in two very interesting papers, 'The Limits of Prediction' (in S. Körner, ed.: *Observation and Interpretation*, 1957, pp. 160 *ff.*) and his inaugural lecture, *Free Will and Determinism Yet Again* (Belfast 1957). I wish to acknowledge my indebtedness to Professor Gallie for drawing, by his criticism, my attention to a lacuna in my argument.

minism) is justified by scientific experience, and that it is no more than a legitimate extrapolation. I have refuted this very important argument for determinism by showing that it does not hold even in a deterministic world. It is clear that this argument must, by its very design, be compatible with other forms of determinism such as the 'third version' suggested. But this does not mean that we have any reason to believe that this third version of determinism is true, or that the world has a structure of the kind described by this third version.

On the contrary, there is every reason to believe that the problem of accountability is sufficient for a rejection of this third version. There is every reason to believe that we cannot collect enough data to *entail* the solution of our prediction task because we do not know what data will be needed for our prediction, even on the assumption that these data 'exist' in the sense that a sufficiently detailed true description of the state of the system would, together with natural laws, entail the prediction. But this could be answered by introducing a fourth version: that a true and sufficiently detailed description, if available, would always entail the solution of any prediction task.

But it is clear that this fourth version, at least, is completely metaphysical. It operates with an existential assumption which is in principle irrefutable: the assumption of the *existence* of a true description which we do not know how to obtain.

To sum up, it was not my aim here to refute the 'third version', which does not seem to be refutable by *pure logic* since a very simple mechanical world seems to be logically possible. My aim was simply to show that the undoubted success of scientific prediction must not be used as an argument in support of a determinist cosmology: in support of the conjecture that *our world* is of the character suggested by the 'third version'.

The way in which 'scientific' determinism has been refuted here seems to me quite interesting. Not only does it show that *we cannot replace our decisions by scientific predictions* about our own future actions (since predictions of this kind are impossible); it also shows that the decisive argument for indeterminism is the existence of rational knowledge itself. We are 'free' (or whatever you want to call it), not because we are subject to chance rather than to strict natural laws, but because the progressive rationalization of the world—the attempt to catch the world in the net of knowledge—has limits, at any moment, in the growth of knowledge itself which, of course, is also a process that belongs to the world.

Rational action without some foreknowledge—of a scientific, a hypothetical, kind at least—is impossible; and it is this very same foreknowledge which turns out to be so limited as to leave room for action—that is, for 'free' action.

24. *An Argument of St. Augustine's, Descartes's, and Haldane's.*

It seems to me that our refutation of 'scientific' determinism has a certain connection with an argument of J.B.S. Haldane's. Similar but somewhat weaker arguments have been propounded by Descartes and, earlier still, by St. Augustine.[1]

The point of the argument is, in Descartes's version, that *a critical grasp of truth,* and a proper assessment of an argument, must be a free, voluntary action of ours (rather than the reaction of a recording machine); as Descartes indicates, perseverance in error and prejudice may consist in a failure or in a refusal to act thus freely—in permitting oneself to be determined uncritically by, say, accepted teaching, and so to remain under the sway of indoctrination.

A similar idea was brilliantly and clearly expressed by Haldane; not as a criticism of determinism, to be sure, but as a criticism of materialism. 'I am not myself a materialist', Haldane wrote, 'because if materialism is true, it seems to me that we cannot

---

[1] J.B.S. Haldane, *The Inequality of Man,* 1932 (reprinted, Pelican Books, 1937; *cp.* p. 157); Descartes, *Principles of Philosophy,* pt. i, sections 36–9 (*cp.* especially the end of 37); St. Augustine, *De libero arbitrio,* book i, especially chapters 11 and 12; book ii, especially chapters 2, 3 and 19. [See Popper's further discussion of this matter in *The Self and Its Brain,* pp. 75–81, where Haldane's recantation is also discussed. Ed.]

know that it is true. If my opinions are the result of the chemical processes going on in my brain, they are determined by the laws of chemistry, not those of logic.' It is obvious that what Haldane criticizes here is not only the idea of materialism (which is, historically, the most important version of 'scientific' determinism) but rather the idea of 'scientific' determinism itself. For it does not matter whether we refer to the laws of mechanics and chemistry or to natural laws in general. The conclusion is the same: if my opinions are fully determined by natural laws and initial conditions, then they are not determined by the laws of logic. (Here, and in Haldane's passage, 'logic' means not only formal logic, but something like the art of argument, and of the rational weighing of evidence.)

Against Haldane's argument it may be said that a mechanical calculating machine, which we may assume to be determined in its working by the laws of physics, nevertheless can work according to the laws of logic. Nor does there seem to be any fundamental difficulty in constructing machines which collect empirical evidence, and act upon it. (Any self-registering thermometer collects observational evidence, and any thermostat acts upon such evidence.) This seems to refute Haldane's argument.

But this seeming refutation misses the point. At any rate, it does not apply to a similar argument which I published not long ago.[2] My argument is based upon a distinction between four different functions of the human language: (1) the *expressive function,* or language considered as symptomatic of the state of the organism; (2) the *signal function,* or language considered as stimulating responses in other organisms; (3) the *descriptive function,* or language considered as describing states of affairs (whether existing or non-existing) and (4) the *argumentative function,* or language considered as a means of rational criticism (as opposed, for example, to mere counter-assertion).[3] The first

[2] *Cp.* my 'Language and the Body-Mind Problem', *Proc. of the XIth International Congress of Philosophy* 7, 1953, pp. 101 *ff.* See also my paper 'A Note on the Body-Mind Problem: Reply to Professor Wilfred Sellars', in *Analysis,* N.S. 15, 1955, pp. 131 *ff.* [Both essays are reprinted in *Conjectures and Refutations,* pp. 293–303. Ed.]

[3] The first three of these functions were distinguished by Karl Bühler,

two are also functions of all animal languages. The last two may be labelled 'higher' functions: they give rise to the idea of a *true* or *false* description, and of a *valid* or *invalid* argument. (I believe that we may distinguish further functions of language—such as prescriptive or advisory or exhortative functions.)

My thesis, briefly, is this. We cannot, admittedly, describe or argue without expressing and signalling as well. But although the descriptive and argumentative functions involve the two lower functions, they are nevertheless *not reducible* to the two lower functions.

By this I mean that although we may well say that describing is a special mode of expressing oneself, and of signalling, it is not *only* this. For the *truth of a description* is something different from, say, the *adequacy of an expression,* or of a reaction to a stimulus; and it is also different from the *adequacy of a signal* to a certain situation, or from its efficiency in evoking a response appropriate to the situation. For a description may be true in fact, even though it was made with the intention to deceive, or to dissimulate; and it may be true in fact even though it was never believed by anybody, and even though it never succeeded in evoking an adequate response.

The argumentative function is likewise not reducible to the two lower functions—expressing and signalling—even though all arguments express and signal. For the validity of an argument cannot be reduced to, say, its persuasive efficiency (which would be a reduction to efficient signalling): a valid argument may fail to persuade anybody; just as invalid arguments have persuaded many people, for many centuries.

Thus description and argumentation are not merely expressions and signals. But a deterministic theory of language in terms of natural laws can explain only these two lower functions: it must conceive all language as symptomatic, and all responses to it

Sprachtheorie, 1934, pp. 25–8; I have added the fourth in 'Towards a Rational Theory of Tradition', *The Rationalist Annual,* January 1949. [Reprinted in *Conjectures and Refutations,* pp. 120–35. See also Popper's discussion of these four functions of language in *The Self and Its Brain,* pp. 57–60; and in *Unended Quest,* pp. 72–8. Ed.]

as responses to signals. The same holds of any theory which appeals to machines. A calculating machine reacts to signals received; and the results which it calculates are expressions, or symptoms, of its internal states. From the point of view of 'scientific' determinism, they cannot be anything else. The difference between a machine which uses a *valid* method of calculation or argument, and one which uses an invalid method, is beyond the horizon of any theory which confines itself to the causal approach of 'scientific' determinism.

'Scientific' determinism is therefore bound either to ignore the difference between the 'higher' and the 'lower' functions of language, or to assert the reducibility of the higher to the lower functions; but both these ways are unacceptable, especially since they cannot do justice to the function and structure of argument.

These views seem to me free of the peculiar metaphysical or *ad hominem* character of Descartes's and Haldane's reasoning; they can be defended at length (I do not intend to do so here) on rational grounds, as parts of a non-metaphysical theory of language. Nevertheless, they have led me to arguments similar to those of Descartes and Haldane: after asserting that the two higher functions cannot be accounted for by 'such philosophies as behaviourism, . . . epiphenomenalism, psycho-physical parallelism, the two-language solutions, physicalism, and materialism'—that is to say, by theories which try to maintain 'the causal completeness of the physical world'—I added: 'All these are *self-defeating* in so far as they establish—unintentionally, of course—the *non-existence of arguments.*'[4] Clearly, the same may be said of 'scientific' determinism. Starting from the power of human reason to predict the world—a power which it conceives as unlimited in principle—it leaves in its conclusion no room for rational argument, for our discernment between truth and falsity, for the difference between brainwashing and learning.

This is precisely Haldane's point. It is the assertion that, if 'scientific' determinism is true, we cannot, in a rational manner,

---

[4] 'Language and the Body-Mind Problem', 3.6 (*loc. cit.*, pp. 103 *ff.*; italics not in the original).

know that it is true; we believe it, or disbelieve it, but not because we freely judge the *arguments or reasons* in its favour to be sound, but because we happen to be so determined (so brainwashed) as to believe it, or not to believe it, or even to believe that we judge it, and accept it, rationally.

This somewhat strange argument does not, of course, refute the doctrine of 'scientific' determinism. Even if it is accepted as valid, the world may still be as described by 'scientific' determinism. But by pointing out that, if 'scientific' determinism is true, we cannot know it, or rationally discuss it, Haldane has given a refutation of the idea from which 'scientific' determinism springs. He has not refuted the doctrine pure and simple, but he has certainly refuted the doctrine *in conjunction with its philosophical background.* He has refuted it in its spirit, as it were, which is the spirit of rationalism or of scientific humanism. For he has shown, I think, that 'scientific' determinism reduces rationality to an illusion. It entails the self-refutation of an over-optimistic view of human reason.

My argument from the impossibility of self-prediction, discussed in the preceding sections, and Haldane's argument have the following in common: they both operate with the idea of rationality and try to show that there is a logical difficulty in considering rationality as pre-determined, or as rationally predictable. In other respects, the two arguments are somewhat different.

CHAPTER IV

METAPHYSICAL ISSUES

25. *The Metaphysical Doctrines of Determinism and Indeterminism.*

By showing the impossibility of predicting the growth of knowledge, I have shown no more than the impossibility of complete prediction *from within* the world. This leaves the possibility open that the world, with everything in it, is completely determined if seen *from without*—perhaps by the Deity. The metaphysical doctrine of determinism should therefore now be considered more closely.

Is metaphysical determinism arguable? I believe it is. At first sight one might be tempted to say that Haldane's argument (or my argument from the four functions of language) establishes the contrary, since it shows that determinism leaves no room for rationality. But this would betray a threefold misunderstanding.

The first misunderstanding is this. Haldane's argument does not necessarily apply to religious determinism (and therefore not to all forms of metaphysical determinism); for just as a teacher, helped by his superior reasoning powers, may often be able to predict the result of rational deliberations in a child without thereby reducing the child's rationality to an illusion, so God might have foreknowledge of our rational decisions without destroying thereby their rationality. It is only the idea of predetermination by *laws of nature* (which have no reasoning power) which turns out to be incompatible with rationality. Thus some forms of metaphysical determinism are affected by Haldane's argument, but not all.

The second misunderstanding is this. Haldane's argument shows that some forms of metaphysical determinism entail the illusionary character of reason. But this creates a difficulty only for those who believe in the difference between reasoned argument and, say, uncritical indoctrination; that is to say, for rationalists. For them, the difficulty may be insurmountable; but other metaphysical determinists may see in Haldane's argument simply a refutation of rationalism rather than of determinism.

Thirdly, Haldane's argument must not be interpreted as establishing the irrationality of any deterministic doctrine, or the impossibility of discussing any such doctrine rationally; on the contrary, it proves, by its very existence, that it is possible to argue about determinism; for it certainly is an argument against it. Similarly, my first two attempts here in this section to defend metaphysical determinism against the allegation that it is not arguable show that there exist not only arguments against metaphysical determinism but also arguments in its defence.

Thus metaphysical determinism is certainly arguable. But the arguments for or against it can never be conclusive: those in its favour must be inconclusive because it is impossible to disprove the existence of an undetermined event in the world. (Here the logical situation is similar to that of any universal theory.) And those against it cannot be conclusive because, for example, we cannot disprove the existence of a spirit who obtains full fore-knowledge about the world from without the world.[1]

---

[1] Metaphysical determinism in its religious form might be formulated by the assertion, 'There exists a spirit who knows now every event of the future'; and in what might be called its quasi-scientific form (i.e., without the demand of predictability from within) by the assertion, 'There exists a theoretical system which, in conjunction with a true description of the present state of the world, entails every event of the future'. (There are, of course, other ways of formulating this idea.) Metaphysical indeterminism can be expressed in a similar form 'There exist events in the future such that no spirit knows them in advance (and no theoretical system conjoined with a description of the present state of the world entails them).' It may be remarked that, if we put any one of these theories in a form $(Ex)\ (y)\ F(x,y)$', its negation will be of the form $(x)\ (Ey)\ \overline{F}(x,y)$'; but this latter formula may be strengthened into $(Ey)\ (x)\ \overline{F}(x,y)$—as indicated in my verbal formulations—without of course changing its metaphysical character; moreover, the stronger formulation may have certain intuitive advantages; as indeed it has, in our case.)

Thus both metaphysical determinism and metaphysical indeterminism are irrefutable. How then can their cases be argued?

In the past, the main argument in favour of metaphysical determinism was based either upon religious grounds or upon faith in 'scientific' determinism. By criticizing the arguments in favour of 'scientific' determinism, I have, indirectly, undermined metaphysical determinism also. Moreover, the argument that the determinist should carry the burden of proof (by 'proof' I do not mean here a conclusive proof, of course) applies not only to 'scientific' determinism but also to its metaphysical version. And so do some of my philosophical arguments, for example, the one from the asymmetry between the past and the future; or Haldane's argument, even though it does not apply to all variants of metaphysical determinism such as religious determinism. None of these arguments are conclusive. But their impact may nevertheless be felt.

26. *Why I Reject Metaphysical Determinism: A Conversation with Parmenides.*

In view of our discussion of special relativity, it may be asked how Einstein himself could have been a convinced determinist. The answer is that, though he may have believed in 'scientific' determinism in his formative years, in his later life his determinism was frankly of a religious or metaphysical kind.[1]

He saw clearly that there was no valid argument leading from experiment to theory; and no doubt he saw as clearly that there was no valid argument leading from science to metaphysics. But he argued in the opposite direction. He did not base his metaphysical determinism upon the *prima facie* deterministic character of his physical theories, but he demanded from his physical theories that they should have this character[2] because he

---

[1] [But see foonote 2 to Chapter I of this volume of the *Postscript,* where it is noted that Einstein apparently abandoned determinism prior to his death. Ed.]

[2] [See footnote 2 to Chapter I of this volume, where Pauli reports that by 1954 Einstein no longer required of his theories that they be 'rigorously deterministic'. Ed.]

believed that physical reality itself was deterministic. (Similarly, he demanded that our theories should be simple because he believed in the simplicity of the world, of physical reality.)

He found my arguments against 'scientific' determinism interesting, and felt that they approached the problem from an angle he had not previously considered. But he felt that, even if my arguments against 'scientific' determinism were valid, they would not shake his metaphysical determinism, or his preference for *prima facie* deterministic theories. I therefore tried a more direct attack upon his metaphysical determinism.

I made it in a private conversation, the day after I had read a paper on this subject.[3] I first tried to describe his own metaphysical determinism, and he agreed with my account of it. I called him 'Parmenides', since he believed in a four-dimensional block-universe, unchanging like the three-dimensional block-universe of Parmenides.[4] (The fourth dimension was time, of course.) He completely agreed with this account of his views, and with the motion picture analogy: in the eyes of God, the film was just there, and the future was there as much as the past: nothing ever happened in this world, and change was a human illusion, as was also the difference between the future and the past.[5]

I attacked this view with two arguments.

The first was that nothing in our experience of this world warranted a Parmenidean metaphysics of this kind. Einstein admitted this, though he was not much impressed until I

---

[3] He was kind enough to attend when I read this paper at Princeton in 1950 (on the lines of my paper on 'Indeterminism' referred to in the first footnote to this chapter). [See Popper's account of this meeting in *Unended Quest*, pp. 128–32. Ed.]

[4] *Cp.* my paper, 'On the Nature of Philosophical Problems and their Roots in Science', *The British Journal for the Philosophy of Science* 3, No. 10, the last paragraph on pp. 141 f. [Reprinted in *Conjectures and Refutations*, pp. 66–96. Ed.]

[5] Of course, the four-dimensional presentation of the world is only a *façon de parler*—or an equivalent language, though a more convenient one for certain purposes than the ordinary language of three dimensions (plus time); it has no necessary metaphysical *implications* (not even as to the past and the future). And yet, it is particularly *suggestive* of a deterministic metaphysics—of immovability in the eyes of God.

reminded him that he had used, quite recently, an analogous argument—that nothing in our experience warranted the introduction of action at a distance—against an attempt to save a certain interpretation of quantum theory.[6]

My second argument was of a more metaphysical nature; it was this. If the universe was assumed to be predetermined like the film, and four-dimensional like the film (for if we take each of its shots as representing a three-dimensional aspect of the world, we may take *the order of the sequence of the shots* as the fourth dimension), then a number of consequences followed which were hard to accept. I pointed out three of them. The first was that the future, being causally entailed by the past, could be viewed as contained in the past, just as the chick is contained in its egg. Einstein's determinism made it *completely* contained in the past, in every single detail. The future became, therefore, *redundant. It was superfluous.* There was little sense in watching a film all of whose shots were strictly logically entailed (in conjunction with a known theory) by its first shot. Moreover, this colossal redundancy was difficult to reconcile with Einstein's idea of simplicity, in its metaphysical sense.

Another consequence was that we were bound to interpret our own human way of *experiencing change,* and the flow of time. This would have to be done, again, by using the film analogy: we experience successive shots or 'time-slices' (using a term due to J. H. Woodger) of our surrounding world, plus their successive order. But this amounts to saying that the arrow of time is subjective, and that time as we experience it is an illusion—a view which forms an integral part of an idealistic or subjectivistic philosophy, and which is linked up with further idealistic and subjectivistic consequences. But one of Einstein's deepest convictions was his realism.

The last consequence, as I pointed out, looked very much like a flat contradiction. If we were experiencing successive shots of an unchanging world, then one thing, at least, was genuinely

---

[6] *Cp.* Albert Einstein, 'Quanten-Mechanik und Wirklichkeit', *Dialectica* 2, 1948, No. 7–8, pp. 320 *ff.*; see especially the last paragraph, p. 323.

changing in this world: our conscious experience. A motion picture film, although existing now, and predetermined, has to *pass,* to *move,* through the projector (that is, relative to ourselves), in order to produce the experience, or the illusion, of temporal change. Similarly, we should have to move, relatively to the four-dimensional block-universe; for the conversion of our future into our past means a change *for us.* And since we are part of the world, there would thus be change in the world—which contradicts Parmenides's view.

These criticisms, I admitted, were perhaps not unanswerable, but an effective answer would not be easy. It would not help to look at our own consciousness as spread out in time, and co-existing in time: we should, again, have to explain why it was not experienced in this way, but rather as a temporal succession of 'time-slices'. Change was real, and could not be explained away without adopting an idealist view of the world—without distinguishing, with Parmenides, between a reality which does not change and an illusionary world of appearance which does change. And even then, we should have to explain the objective fact—the reality—of the illusion, and our inability to get rid of it, even if we accept its illusionary character. (In the case of most optical illusions, knowledge that we are suffering from an illusion likewise fails to dispel it: the illusion is a fact; and indeed, a fact which in many cases can be explained physiologically.)

In view of all these difficulties, I pointed out that by far the simplest way was to reject any metaphysical view which did not allow for the asymmetry between the past and the future, and to accept a view which would allow the future not to be entailed by, or in some sense contained in, the past; in other words, to accept an indeterminist view of the world. Indeterminist metaphysics seemed to be closer to experience, and did not seem to create new difficulties of any kind—once the arguments in favour of 'scientific' determinism had been shown to be invalid.

These were my arguments. Parmenides discussed them with great patience, as was his wont. He said that he was impressed by them, and that he had no answer for them. Beyond this, I did not pursue the matter.

27. *The Gain for Science: A Theory of Propensities.*

So far I have criticized determinism by trying to show its disadvantages. I have also hinted that its abandonment would produce some positive gains for common sense, ethics, the philosophy of science, cosmology and, I hope, for truth.

But in this book, and in the present context, with quantum theory as one of our main interests (see *Quantum Theory and the Schism in Physics,* Vol. III of this *Postscript),* a gain—and perhaps a major gain—to science itself provides perhaps the strongest positive argument in favour of indeterminism: in rejecting determinism, we open the way for an approach that could be of real significance for science. I have in mind a physical interpretation of probability theory in the form of a physical theory of propensities. (See *Realism and the Aim of Science,* Vol. I of this *Postscript,* Part 2.)

Even if such a theory, after serious discussion, ultimately proves unacceptable, the fact will remain that only by discarding determinism do we gain the freedom necessary for a serious consideration of the propensity interpretation as a physical theory. Thus determinism is not only unsupported by argument; it prevents us from seriously considering possibilities—such as the idea of physical propensities—which, however their merits may ultimately be assessed, are certainly worthy of being so considered.

The idea of physical propensities can best be explained by analogy with that of physical forces. A physical force is an unobservable but testable hypothetical entity; testable, of course, by testing a hypothesis that involves a force. For example, the hypothesis of the presence, in a certain place, of an electrostatic force of a certain direction and intensity can be tested by its predictable effects—the direction and magnitude of the acceleration of a test body which may be put in that place.

Now let us assume that in a sequence of tests each yields the same results: we may explain this by the hypothesis that the force is constant. Let us assume, on the other hand, that in a sequence of tests each yields the same results as to the direction of the force but that the results concerning the magnitude of the acceleration fluctuate: then we may explain this by the hypothesis that the direction of this force is constant while its intensity fluctuates. A corresponding interpretation may be given in case the direction of the acceleration fluctuates but not its magnitude.

But in certain cases it may turn out that these hypotheses of fluctuating forces are theoretically unsatisfactory; for example, because we have kept all the conditions during the test as constant as we could. In this case, we may perhaps explain the fluctuations as due to unknown disturbances, or unknown sources of failure to keep the experimental conditions constant. But this too may be unsatisfactory, and we may then decide to introduce a new idea. We may say that the *objective situation*, all of whose conditions we have kept constant, determines *propensities rather than forces*; that it determines propensities to accelerate—or propensities to become accelerated—which may be highest near the mean of the accelerations, and taper out towards both higher and lower values. The hypothesis of the presence of such propensities would have to be tested by statistical tests (as indicated in Volume I, Part 2 of the *Postscript,* on probability).

This idea can only be introduced, of course, once we have given up determinism; for the assumption is that *the same situation may produce fluctuating results.* It is clear from our discussion that, if we do not give up determinism, we may have to operate with the idea of fluctuating forces instead of the idea of propensities; and it is also clear that, in certain cases, the two explanations may turn out to be mathematically equivalent. Which, then, shall we accept?

An answer to this question cannot be given with anything like assurance, but questions of testability may be decisive. The determinist interpretation in terms of fluctuating forces will have to postulate *fluctuating initial conditions.* If this postulate can be tested, and stands up to tests, the determinist's explanation in terms of fluctuating forces wins. If, however, the determinist is driven to resort to an untestable hypothesis of *hidden fluctuations of the initial conditions,* an explanation in terms of propensities whose presence can be tested statistically may become preferable. (Other circumstances which may make it preferable will be discussed in the next section.) In any case, a prejudice in favour of the doctrine of determinism should not be allowed to stand in the way of a free discussion of the theory of propensities.

I have tried to explain the idea of propensity as a kind of generalization of—or perhaps even an alternative to—the idea of force, mainly because the idea of force was also at first viewed with suspicion by rationalist physicists who rightly denounced it as occult and metaphysical. But since then we have learned (or so I hope) that physical science explains the known by the un-known,[1] and the visible world by a hypothetical invisible world; and we have got used to the idea of forces. (Newton was never quite happy about the idea of an attractive force; Heinrich Hertz tried to do without it; and so did Einstein.) Thus we may likewise get used to that of propensities.

In drawing an analogy between propensities and forces, I do not wish to suggest that we should consider only, or mainly, propensities to accelerate or to be accelerated. On the contrary, other propensities may be of greater importance; in general, we consider propensities to assume, under given conditions, one or another of a set of 'possible' (or 'virtual') states.

The numerical values of the propensities to take up different states may vary from state to state. The function (probability distribution) which determines these values will in general reflect the symmetries or asymmetries of the conditions. An analogy with forces may come in at two points: we may have to consider the propensities (or perhaps other functions closely related to them) as hypothetical physical magnitudes, capable even of interaction (or perhaps interference) like forces. And we may have to attribute weights to the propensities: weights that, though in accordance with the symmetries inherent in the situation, may yet not be fully determined by these symmetries alone.

---

[1] For the idea of explaining the known by the unknown, see my papers 'The Nature of Philosophical Problems and their Roots in Science', *The British Journal of the Philosophy of Science* 3, 1952, pp. 124 *ff.*, especially 144, 148 *ff.*, and 'Three Views Concerning Human Knowledge' in *Contemporary British Philosophy*, III, ed. by H. D. Lewis, 1956. [Both are reprinted in *Conjectures and Refutations*. See also Volume I of this *Postscript*, section 15. Ed.]

28. Prima facie *Deterministic Theories and Probabilistic Theories.*

Prima facie deterministic theories cannot answer all the questions which can legitimately be asked in physics. They cannot answer such simple questions as 'How is it that a mixing machine always succeeds in mixing up, say, coffee beans and cocoa beans which were put into it in two separate heaps?'; or the very similar question, 'How is it that an appropriately constructed penny-tossing machine into which we put pennies, always in precisely the same way, produces sequences of penny-tosses of a random character?'[1] Clearly, these are physical problems which cannot be dismissed; and since they ask what are essentially *statistical questions,* they must be answered by what are essentially statistical or probabilistic theories.

Perhaps the most characteristic and most important of these problems in physics are those of the intensity of spectral lines and those of the half life of radioactively decaying nuclei.

In the body of *L.Sc.D.,* I asserted on many occasions that (synthetic) statistical conclusions can be obtained only from statistical premises. In view of my later work on probability (see Volume I, Part 2, of *The Postscript*), this has to be reformulated.

I use the word *'probabilistic'* in a wide sense here, so as to cover 'objective' theories which are either statistical theories (theories about sequences) or theories asserting a probability in the sense of set-theoretical probability or of the propensity interpretation. (I do not here consider subjective theories, or 'inductive' probabilities in the sense of, say, Jeffreys or Keynes or Carnap.[2])

In this usage, my old assertion—that statistical conclusions can be obtained only from statistical premises—can be replaced by the following:

(1) Probabilistic conclusions (more precisely, non-analytic

---

[1] An important step in this direction was taken by Khinchine; see *Sowjet-wissenschaft* 1954, pp. 268 *ff.* He calls his method 'the method of arbitrary distribution functions'. (My attention has been drawn to this paper by Dr I. Lakatos.)

[2] See *Realism and the Aim of Science,* Volume I of this *Postscript,* Part 2.

statements asserting probabilities or frequencies other than 0 or 1) can be derived only from probabilistic premises.

(2) Statistical conclusions can be derived from statistical or from other probabilistic premises. If derived from non-statistical probabilistic premises, statistical conclusions do not, strictly speaking, follow; but by interpreting the probabilities or measures 0 and 1 as 'almost never' or 'almost always', we may say that statistical conclusions 'almost follow' from non-statistical probabilistic premises.

In view of (2) we may sometimes be able to *test* probabilistic theories by testing statistical statements which *'almost follow'* from the probabilistic premises. For example, we may test by a sequence of trials the theory that the probability of tossing heads with a certain machine equals ½; for on the assumption that the probability of tossing heads is ½, and that the tosses are independent, so that the probability is constant, the probability for a sequence of trials not to be a random-like sequence with the frequency ½ will be zero; whence it further follows that most long-observed sequences will very nearly 'realize' the frequency properties of a random sequence or collective.

This example is only intended to remind the reader how statistical assumptions may 'almost' follow from non-statistical probabilistic premises. It is in no way intended as an answer to the question, raised at the beginning of this section, of how to explain the observable effects achieved by a mixing machine, or (what amounts to more or less the same) by a penny-tossing machine.

A deterministic attempt to answer these questions may be made by combining a *prima facie* deterministic theory of the physical processes involved with an assumption concerning the initial conditions; an assumption which might be described as *a probabilistic assumption about 'hidden' initial conditions*.

To explain this more fully with the help of an example, let us assume that our penny-tossing machine is constructed with very great precision, so as to repeat, or to reproduce, its own movements very exactly. The penny, let us assume, is several times picked up by the machine, held in a strictly vertical position, spun round a vertical axis, and then allowed to drop,

97

while still spinning, on to an inclined plane which it either rolls down, or slides down (if it falls on its side before it comes to the end of the plane). The process is repeated, say, twenty times, after which the penny is ejected.

How do we explain the fact that a machine of this kind will succeed in turning out a very well 'mixed' or 'random' sequence of pennies, with about half showing heads and half tails? We can hardly attribute this fact to any irregularity in the manner of feeding the penny into the machine, for (a) if we feed it into the machine always in the same way, as exactly as we can, the statistical result is unaffected and (b) if we vary our method of feeding, the statistical result is also unaffected. Moreover, we can build the machine so that, in its early procedures, it corrects with great precision any differences in the position of the penny which may exist when it is first fed into the machine: it can thus *equalize* the initial conditions (though of course not completely).

In view of all this, we may be inclined to attribute the statistical result to minute and *hidden differences in the state of the machine and the penny*—for example, to molecular or atomic changes; that is to say, we may attribute the differences in the result to differences in the hidden initial conditions. We then can explain the different macroscopic result by pointing out that the machine contains a device (such as dropping the spinning penny several times vertically, in our example; or in another machine, shaking it violently) which amounts to an amplification of minute hidden differences that are bound to occur in the various runs of the machine.

This explains—I believe, quite satisfactorily—the fact that the machine does not always produce heads, but sometimes tails. But it is insufficient to explain the statistical *stability* of the result—the fact that the observed output of the machine is in very close agreement with the hypothesis that it yields a collective, with the relative frequency $\frac{1}{2}$, say.[3]

[3] The machine might show a 'bias' and produce frequencies which are greater than $\frac{1}{2}$; or it might periodically change its frequencies between, say, 0.45 and 0.55 (in which case the periods would have to be fairly long in order to be ascertainable).

In order to explain this, we must assume (i) that the sequence of the hidden initial conditions also forms a collective. And this, in its turn, may be further explained by assuming (ii) that any assumption other than (i) is highly improbable—that the set of initial conditions which do *not* form a chance-like collective has the probability or measure zero.[4] In this way, our statistical problem is solved, ultimately, by a deduction from a probabilistic but non-statistical assumption about the hidden initial conditions. Or in other words, our statistical problem was solved by a probabilistic theory; for the *prima facie* deterministic theory of the machine plays only a very subordinate part in the explanation of the *statistical* effect.

I consider an explanation of the kind here given as satisfactory up to a point; but it is important to realize that it operates not with a purely statistical theory, but with a probability or measure theory. For we *explained* the assumption—marked above by '(i)'—that the initial conditions form a chance-like collective by the further assumption—marked by '(ii)'—that the occurrence of any other sequence would have zero probability or measure. This means, however, that we assume that a non-statistical measure theory of probability holds for the distribution of our initial conditions, and that *this* probability theory has to be physically interpreted (by propensities, I suggest).

A purely statistical theory would not help. It would mean stopping at (i), and therefore *explaining* the random-like character of the sequence of the (observable) penny tosses by *assuming* the same character for the sequence of the hidden initial conditions. But this only shifts the issue one step back. Moreover, some of these latter sequences may well in fact be random-like; but what right have we to predict (as we do) that they will all be so, or almost all—as a *rule*, as a matter of *law*?

---

[4] Thus we should have to show, for example, that almost all (that is, *all* but for a set of the measure zero) initial states of a gas lead to equilibrium states (or to a Maxwellian distribution of the velocities of the molecules). All these are probabilistic tasks, and tasks which have been, or are being, solved. But the solution makes sense only if we interpret the measure zero as a propensity zero.

29. *Landé's Blade.*

No physicist that I know of has seen this problem more clearly, or done more to show what is involved here, than Alfred Landé. His argument[1] is designed to show that we must accept probabilities of single events as fundamental, and as irreplaceable by any statement except by other probability statements. Moreover, his argument shows that even if we combine a *prima facie* deterministic theory with statistical assumptions concerning initial conditions, we only get an infinite regress; and an interpretation which sticks to this assumption is bound to become untestable, metaphysical (or 'purely academic', in Landé's terminology). I will quote Landé's important passage (which, incidentally, also contains an argument against determinism) in full.

> Ivory balls are dropped through a tube on the centre of a steel blade, and a 50:50 average ratio of balls falling to the right [*r*] and left [*l*] is observed. Now, although a superficial observer may consider an individual *r*-event as purely accidental, a more skillful physicist may be able to see in advance that an *r*-ball even before hitting the blade possessed a slight preponderance to the right. This seeing in advance presupposes that the observer has an optical device, a sort of optical blade, doing the same job of distinguishing between *r*- and *l*-balls which the steel blade does later. One of the events in the life of an *r*-ball may have been a predestined encounter with a group of molecules when leaving the tube. According to the classical view, then, today's *r*-state is preceded by yesterday's *r*-state back to the infinite past through a continuous chain of events . . . *rrr* . . . of which the steel blade encounter is only one link.
>
> When the determinist is now asked for a causal explanation of the average 50:50 ratio between *r*- and *l*-balls his answer will be that *this ratio, too, was predetermined* long before the tube and the blade ever existed. Pressed further [to explain] why even the fluctuations from

[1] See Alfred Landé, 'Probability in Classical and Quantum Theory', *Scientific Papers Presented to Max Born*, 1953, pp. 58 *ff.*, and Alfred Landé, *Foundations of Quantum Theory*, 1955, pp. 3 *ff.* [See also Landé's *From Dualism to Unity in Quantum Physics*, 1960, pp. 3–8; and *New Foundations of Quantum Mechanics*, 1965, pp. 29–32. Ed.]

the average conform with statistical expectations of the theory of random events, he may retreat into conceding a *pre-established harmony* between groups of events looking *as if* subjected to random fluctuations although *in reality* each single event was predetermined. However, this would put the "as if" and the "reality" in an upside-down position. The random distribution is a physical reality, and . . . [a determinist system] which merely looks like random is a purely academic construction. A distribution of effects satisfying the . . . error theory requires, . . . from the determinist's viewpoint, a corresponding random distribution of causes at an earlier time, and from there back to a still earlier time. A programme of giving a strictly deterministic theory of statistically distributed events leads nowhere.

Landé's simple but beautiful argument may be made even more explicit.

(a) Let us assume that the number N of the balls dropped was 1,000. The determinist, as Landé points out, can explain both, the 50:50 ratio of the results and the random fluctuation, only by the assumption that there was a corresponding distribution in the initial conditions of each of the 1,000 single events. If he tries to explain why these 1,000 initial conditions show the 50:50 ratio and the random fluctuations, he is, clearly, on the way to an infinite regress. If he refuses to try to give an explanation, he has to accept the facts as unexplained, as miraculous.

But he may be pressed even further: he will no doubt conjecture—or if he does not, others will—that the next 1,000 events, or the next 10,000 events, will yield closely similar statistical results. Thus he will have to conjecture that they too will be due to a corresponding distribution of initial conditions; and he will be unable to say why he conjectures that these ratios will be so strangely stable. (In this sense, he will again have to believe in a 'pre-established harmony', as Landé puts it.)

What Landé shows here is the emptiness of the old deterministic 'explanation' according to which many small causes or 'errors' will (by partly cancelling each other, etc.) produce the random result. All this may certainly be true; but it does not change the fact that for the determinist, the *statistical results* are derivable, if at all, only from *statistical assumptions* concerning the distribu-

101

tion of the initial conditions. Thus we find that the strangely law-like behaviour of the statistical sequences remains, for the determinist, *ultimately irreducible and inexplicable*. More especially, it cannot be explained by the determinist as due to an element of randomness or chance, or by an appeal to high probabilities: Landé's argument shows that these ideas become inapplicable, since all the determinist can appeal to is the unexplained statistical distribution of the sequence of earlier events (i.e., of the sequence of initial conditions).

These considerations of Landé's strongly suggest that determinists who believe that they can explain statistical behaviour allow considerations of probability (and even of propensity) to slip, unnoticed, into their assumptions. They operate with an assumption which may be called *the general hypothesis of randomness*: the assumption that uncontrolled initial conditions are always random. (This assumption is often called 'the principle of molecular chaos'.) The assumption may again be interpreted in a purely statistical sense—producing the same difficulties as before—or in a propensity sense. In the latter sense, the hypothesis means that (i) the controlled experimental conditions do not absolutely fix the initial conditions but leave them a certain amount of play, and that (ii) each of the possibilities thus left open to the initial conditions will be realized with a certain propensity or probability (which may sometimes be calculated with the help of symmetry considerations). It is one of the merits of Landé's argument to show that these more satisfying considerations have inadvertently crept in, and also that they should have been strictly excluded by those who wish to retain the deterministic framework.

(b) In order to show even more clearly the difficulties in which the determinist lands himself, let us assume that the ratio of the r-balls to the l-balls was not 50:50 but, say, 40:60. In this case, it is reasonable to assume that a minute shift of the blade to the left will improve the ratio in favour of the r-balls. We may perhaps achieve, in consequence of the shift, a ratio-of 52:48, or a 50:50 ratio, and a further slight shift may even give the r-balls the majority.

It will be granted that experiments with results such as these can be made, if only it is granted that we can get stable Landé-frequencies; that is to say, we are all ready to *predict* that small adjustments in the position of the blade will lead to results like those indicated. But for the determinist, predictions of this kind must be impossible, or miraculous, since they would have to assume a 'pre-established harmony' in the initial conditions; he cannot, as we have seen, explain them.

(c) Landé's argument may also be used in order to criticize the doctrine that probability considerations enter into science only if *our knowledge* is insufficient to enable us to make predictions with certainty.

From a determinist point of view, this doctrine is of fundamental importance: it is the only alternative to that theory of irreducible and miraculous statistical distribution of initial conditions which has just been criticized. Obviously, it is the only doctrine which, from a determinist point of view, can make sense of *singular* probability statements. But it seems to be held by many who do not profess determinist views.[2]

In order to see the weakness and even the irrelevance of this doctrine, let us assume again that we are faced with an arrangement as described by Landé, with balls dropping on to a steel blade, and a 50:50 ratio of *r* and *l* balls. Let us further assume that we have an optical blade with the help of which we can *know with certainty* of every oncoming ball whether it will be a right ball or a left ball. This undoubtedly makes it unnecessary to invoke probabilities so far as the prediction of each single ball is concerned. But it does not in any way affect our problem. The balls, we may assume,[3] fall to the right or to the left of the steel blade exactly as before, with the same 50:50 ratio, and with the same statistical fluctuations; and the problem of explaining these

[2] For example, it is held by Pauli (see *Quantum Theory and the Schism in Physics*, Vol. III of this *Postscript*, section 5). It is as a rule held by all those who uphold a subjective or an inductive interpretation of probability. How far the motive for upholding these interpretations springs from an unconscious belief in determinism (as I suspect) is of course difficult to decide.

[3] If the balls are sufficiently heavy, they will be unaffected by our optical blade.

statistical results, and that of explaining our ability to predict that future sequences will lead to similar results (provided the conditions are unchanged), remain precisely the same as before, in spite of the fact that *we now know every single result in advance*.

But does not our advance knowledge of the *r* and *l* balls enable us to change their ratios? We may assume that the balls come through Landé's tube sufficiently slowly, and sufficiently spaced from one another, to observe them with the optical blade and to remove each *r*-ball by hand (putting it in a box, say). As a result, we shall obtain *only l*-balls instead of a 50:50 ratio. Thus on the basis of our precise knowledge, we can *control* our statistical results as we like.

This argument is certainly correct. But we shall still find that the ratio of the *l*-balls to the balls now put away in the box is 50:50, as before; and the problem of explaining this ratio, and the statistical fluctuations, remains unchanged: it has again been merely shifted.

The 50:50 ratio, it will be clear by now, depends upon the objective experimental conditions, and has nothing whatever to do with our knowledge, or lack of it. In so far as we changed the experimental conditions—replacing the *r*-balls by box-balls— there was a change in the results; and in so far as we did not change the conditions, leaving the tube and the blade untouched, there was no change.

30. *Landé's Blade and the Propensity Interpretation.*

We have seen that when we shift the blade, frequencies will change. (*Cp.* (b) in the preceding section.) The task of the theory will be to explain this fact in a simple manner, showing why we may predict these and similar changes (as in fact we do).

Any change of the position of the blade changes the possibilities inherent in the experimental set-up, and its symmetry-conditions. More precisely, it changes the measure of these possibilities: a shift to the left increases the possibility of obtaining *r*-balls. By calling the measures of possibilities objective probabilities or *propensities*, I am merely using another word; but

I do this in order to draw attention to the fact that these 'possibilities' are now considered as *physical magnitudes* which, like forces, can interact and combine, and that they may therefore be considered, in spite of the term 'possibility', as *physically real*: they are not merely logical possibilities, but *physical possibilities*.

The propensities may be interpreted as objective, singular probabilities. They are singular in so far as they are inherent in the experimental set-up which is assumed to be the same for each experiment. (Thus we obtain independence, or freedom from after-effects, for the elements of the sequence.) And they thus manifest themselves in a Bernoullian manner in the frequencies of sequences which are repetitions of the experimental set-up.

If the experimental set-up is such that we always get the same result—for example r balls only—then it may be of a *prima facie* deterministic kind; if it is such that we obtain relative frequencies which are equal neither to 1 nor to 0, then it will be of a probabilistic kind. In every case we may say that the experimental set-up determines the *probabilities* of each single result of the experiment, or the *propensities* to obtain certain results.

Since the conditions are objective physical conditions, the propensities or probabilities are also objective. They should be viewed as properties, not of the system under investigation (the ball, or the electron, or whatever it may be), but as properties of the whole experimental set-up (which includes, of course, the ball, or the electron, i.e., the system under investigation).

Thus I suggest that we admit that propensities may exist—just like forces, or other abstract or 'occult' physical entities, introduced in order to explain the known by the unknown. They are, like forces, the result of (or dependent upon) certain *relations* between other physical entities—say, between physical bodies, or between more abstract entities such as currents, of fields, or perhaps even between other probabilities: once we admit these abstract but objective physical entities (which may be able to change continuously) into our physical theory, there is no reason why we should not allow them to interact, or be linked by laws which, in certain arrangements, make the propensity in one place dependent upon the propensities of its neighbourhood.

105

My old view, developed in *L.Sc.D.* (e.g., section 57), was that statistical results (such as those discussed by Landé) must be explained by statistical hypotheses which, in turn, may be inspired by, but cannot be derived from, symmetry considerations.

This view was criticized by Einstein (in two letters) and also by Jordan.[1] Both would have been right had they merely asserted that I was wrong; but both were wrong in their contention that statistical results can be obtained from classical deterministic assumptions. Probabilistic premises are indeed indispensable for statistical conclusions, though these premises need not be statistical, but may be hypotheses about propensities; and since propensities are measures of possibilities, they may, in certain cases, be validly derived from symmetry considerations (this is the case in Einstein's example), or from the fact that certain possibilities have zero measure (this is the case in Jordan's example).

31. *Conclusion.*

Although I believe that my refutation of 'scientific' determinism is needed to prepare the basis for a full understanding of probability in physics, my own refutation (as distinct from Landé's) nowhere makes use of probability theory; nor do I appeal to quantum theory. 'Free will', too, is mentioned only incidentally. [But see the 'Afterword'.] My argument holds for every physical theory, however strongly deterministic it may appear.

As to its application to human questions, and to the problems of ethics and of responsibility, only a few hints have been given (in sections 15, 16, 23, and 24). All singular events in this world are unique, and if considered under the aspect of their uniqueness, they might be described as undetermined, or 'free'. For some events, this way of describing them is perhaps far-fetched. But when human personalities and their actions are involved, it

---

[1] One of Einstein's letters is printed as Appendix *xii to *L.Sc.D.*; the passage I am alluding to is the last paragraph of the letter. P. Jordan's criticism is to be found in his *Anschauliche Quantentheorie*, 1936, p. 282.

may be the most important aspect for us. It is clearly so whenever we are personally interested in the people concerned.

In so far as man is a predictor, my results about predicting machines are, I believe, *a fortiori* applicable to man and to human society.

'Know thyself'—that is, know your limitations—is an ideal which, we can now see, is logically unrealizable. Since we are calculators, we cannot know ourselves fully, not even all our limitations—at least not those to our knowledge.

But I certainly do not intend to suggest that the parallelism between ourselves and predicting machines goes far. I think that man is not just a predictor, but more. Even in so far as our purely intellectual activities are concerned, we have hopes, fears, interests, and problems. We are not merely calculators, and not mainly calculators; and in so far as we are calculators, we are miserably bad ones. Every ordinary adding machine is superior to most of us. Indeed, we would not construct multiplication tables and systems of arithmetic if our brains could calculate. We construct methods of calculating with pencil and paper, and electronic brains, simply because we have not got enough brains ourselves.

Thus we are not mainly calculators. But we are constructors of calculators. We make them because we are interested in problems whose solutions are beyond our limited calculating powers; and, even more, because we are fascinated by the new problems which the construction of calculators presents to us. Our fundamental intellectual impulse is to search for difficulties—or even to invent difficulties, in order to overcome them.

A calculator may be able to turn out mathematical theorems. It may distinguish proofs from non-proofs—and thereby certain theorems from non-theorems. But it will not distinguish difficult and ingenious proofs and interesting theorems from dull and uninteresting ones. It will thus 'know' too much—far too much—that is without any interest. The knowledge of a calculator, however systematic, is like a sea of truisms in which a few particles of gold—of valuable information—may be suspended. (Catching these particles may be as difficult, and more boring, than trying to get them without a calculator.) It is only man, with his problems, who can lend significance to the calculators' senseless power of producing truths.

To put this argument in a more formal way, it is the function of every theory to divide all statements pertaining to the subject matter in question into three distinct classes—those which the theory asserts to be true, those which it asserts to be false, and those about which it does not make any assertion. It is for this reason that an inconsistent theory is useless; for it does not achieve such a division, but asserts every statement (and therefore also the negation of every statement). An inconsistent theory is useless because it asserts too much.

Now a good (that is, a consistent) calculator is certainly not useless, for it can achieve such a classification. However, it still asserts too much. If somehow or other it is made to derive all the consequences of any theory one after another automatically, then it will still possess no method of picking out the interesting or important ones, nor a method ensuring that it produces even one of these within any definite interval of time. For with every moderately useful statement such as '2 + 1 = 3', it will also contain an infinite sequence of statements '2 + 1 $\neq$ 4', '2 + 1 $\neq$ 5' . . . and other infinite sequences of statements such as '2 + 1 $\neq$ 3 + 1', '2 + 1 $\neq$ 4 + 1'. . . . In the infinite sequence of the statements in their order of production, the probability of hitting upon one which is interesting (by any reasonable standard) will be zero.

Only the human brain [*or perhaps I should have said the human mind] can create interests, purposes, problems and ends—even within the comparatively narrow field of its intellectual activities.

Another argument would be this. We learn by mistakes; and this means that when we arrive at inconsistencies we turn back, and reframe our assumptions. In applying this method we go so far as to re-examine assumptions even of a logical nature, if necessary. (This happened in the case of the logical paradoxes.) It is hardly conceivable that a machine could do the same. If its creators, incautiously, equip it with inconsistencies, then it will derive, in time, every statement that it can form (and its negation). We may perhaps equip it with a gadget which will warn it, in case it derives '0=1', and make it abandon some of its assumptions. But we shall hardly be able to construct a machine which can criticize and readjust its own methods of derivation, or its own methods of criticism.

The general upshot of our considerations appears to be the restoration of the naïve view of the world, described as the 'commonsense view' in section 1—the view that there are events which can be predicted, or which are 'determined', and other events which cannot be predicted and are not 'determined'.

But our considerations even suggest something like a reconciliation between this view and the other—the 'more sophisticated' —view that it is as a rule only lack of knowledge which makes us believe that events are unpredictable.

This reconciliation may be brought about if we realize that the existence of knowledge in the physical world—or rather, of physical events interpretable as representing knowledge, or resulting from knowledge—creates the kind of indeterminism we have been discussing here. Knowledge may conquer new problems. But in doing so, it will create new problems which it cannot solve; at least not at once. For it cannot foreknow its own future conquests.

ADDENDA

INDETERMINISM IS NOT ENOUGH: AN AFTERWORD[1]

My topic here is human freedom. By human freedom I mean what has usually been called 'free will'. I shall however avoid the term 'will', lest discussing it sidetrack us into sterile problems of terminology. For similar reasons I shall not explicitly discuss moral freedom, even though it is the kind of human freedom in which philosophers have interested themselves most frequently. Instead, I will begin by discussing the freedom to create works of art or explanatory theories in science. Moral freedom is of great importance, but again, its discussion is liable to sidetrack us into the problem of moral responsibility or even into the problem of reward and punishment. I hope, however, to simplify my discussion by avoiding any direct discussion of moral issues and by restricting myself to questions of the freedom to create, and the freedom to evaluate reasons or arguments, for or against statements of fact, or scientific theories. Presumably, if we enjoy *this* kind of freedom, we may also enjoy the freedom to create, to reason, and to choose in areas of morality, and to enjoy the responsibility that goes with such creation and choice. Whereas if

[1] [Since writing the *Postscript* over twenty-five years ago, Popper has published several essays relating to issues of determinism and human freedom. One of these, the Arthur Holly Compton Memorial Lecture, 'Of Clouds and Clocks: An Approach to the Problem of Rationality and the Freedom of Man', has been published (as Chapter 6 of *Objective Knowledge*), and is readily available. A second essay, 'Indeterminism Is Not Enough' (first published in *Encounter* 40, April 1973, pp. 20–26), is not so easily available, and makes an important addition to the argument of this book. It is therefore re-published here as a kind of Afterword for this book. Ed.]

we do *not* have at least the freedom to reason and argue about matters of fact, we could hardly have any moral freedom.

The title of this Afterword essay, 'Indeterminism Is Not Enough', is meant to indicate that an indeterministic physics—which it is the concern of the body of this book to defend—is by itself not enough to make room for human freedom: it is not enough to make human freedom understandable. To do this, I assert, we need more. We need in addition at least the *causal openness* of what I am going to call World 1 towards World 2, as well as the *causal openness* of World 2 towards World 3, and *vice versa*. Thus I will begin by explaining what I call World 1, World 2, and World 3.[2]

The Worlds 1, 2, and 3

By 'World 1' I mean what is usually called the world of physics: of rocks, and trees and physical fields of forces. I also mean to include here the worlds of chemistry and biology. By 'World 2' I mean the psychological world. It is studied by students of the human mind, but also of the minds of animals. It is the world of feelings of fear and of hope, of dispositions to act, and of all kinds of subjective experiences, including subconscious and unconscious experiences. Thus the terms 'World 1' and 'World 2' are both easily explained. The explanation of what I call 'World 3' is a little more difficult.

By 'World 3' I mean the world of the products of the human mind. Although I include works of art in World 3 and also ethical values and social institutions (and thus, one might say, societies), I shall confine myself largely to the world of scientific libraries, to books, to scientific problems, and to theories, including mistaken theories.

Books, journals, and libraries belong to both World 1 and

---

[2] [For detailed accounts of Worlds 1, 2, and 3, see K. R. Popper: *Objective Knowledge,* Chapters 3 and 4; and *The Self and Its Brain* (with Sir John Eccles), 1977, Chapter P2. Ed.]

World 3. They are physical objects, and as such belong to World 1: they are subject to the physical restrictions or physical laws of World 1. For example, though two copies of the same book may be physically altogether similar, they cannot take up the same part of physical space; thus they are two different World 1 objects. But they belong not only to World 1: they also belong to World 3. *Two* very similar copies of the same book are *different* as World 1 objects; but if the *contents* of two physically similar (or dissimilar) books are the same, then as World 3 objects, the two books are identical: they are different copies of *one* World 3 object. Moreover, this one World 3 object is subject to the restrictions and the valuations of World 3; it can for instance be examined for its logical consistency, and evaluated for its informative content.

The *content* of a book, or of a theory, is something abstract. All *concrete* physical bodies, such as rocks, trees, animals and human bodies, belong to World 1; and all psychological states, whether conscious or subconscious, belong to World 2. But *abstract* things, such as problems, theories and arguments, including mistaken ones, belong to World 3. (Also inconsistent arguments and theories. This does not, of course, make World 3 inconsistent, for World 3 is neither a theory nor an assertion nor an argument: it is a class of things, a universe of discourse.) Moreover, unless we choose to introduce for works of art, say, a new term such as 'World 4', a play like *Hamlet* and a symphony like Schubert's 'Unfinished' also belong to World 3; and just as an individual copy of a book belongs *both* to World 1 *and* to World 3, so particular performances of *Hamlet* and of Schubert's Unfinished Symphony belong both to World 1 and to World 3. They belong to World 1 in so far as they consist of complex physical events; but they belong to World 3 in so far as they have a content, a message, or a meaning.

The terms 'World 1', 'World 2', and 'World 3' are consciously chosen as being colourless and arbitrary. But there is a historical reason for numbering them 1, 2, and 3: it seems that the physical world existed before the world of animal feelings; and I conjecture that World 3 begins only with the evolution of a specifically human language. I will take the world of *linguistically formulated human knowledge* as being most characteristic of World 3. It is the world of problems, theories and arguments; and I shall also include those problems, theories, and arguments which have not yet been linguistically formulated. I will also assume that World 3 has a history—that certain problems, theories, and arguments were discovered, or perhaps refuted, at certain dates, while others were at those dates still undiscovered, or unrefuted.

The Reality of the Three Worlds

It is, I think, good common sense to accept the reality or existence of the World 1 of physical bodies. As Dr. Johnson's famous refutation of Berkeley shows, a physical body such as a rock can be said to exist because it can be *kicked;* and if you kick a rock hard enough, you will feel that it can kick back. Following Alfred Landé, I propose to say that something exists, or is real, if and only if it can be kicked and can, in principle, kick back; to put it a little more generally, I propose to say that something exists, or is real, if and only if it can *interact* with members of World 1, with hard, physical, bodies.

Thus, World 1, or the physical world, may be taken as the standard example of reality or of existence. However, I believe in the insignificance of questions of terminology or of the usage or meaning of words. Thus I regard the usage of words like 'real' or 'existing' as not very important; especially if compared with questions about the *truth* of theoretical assertions or propositions.

The proposition the truth of which I wish to defend and which seems to me to go a little beyond common sense is that not only are the physical World 1 and the psychological World 2 real but so also is the abstract World 3; *real* in exactly that sense in which the physical World 1 of rocks and trees is real: the objects of World 2 and of World 3 can kick each other, as well as the physical objects of World 1; and they can also be kicked back.

116

The Reality of Worlds 1 and 2

Although I propose, with Dr Johnson, Alfred Landé, and other commonsense realists, to regard World 1 as the very standard of reality, I am not a monist but a pluralist.[3] A monistic immaterialism or phenomenalism that denies the existence of World 1 and admits only experiences as existing, thus only World 2, was fairly fashionable until quite recently. At present, the opposite view is much more fashionable. I mean the view that *only* World 1 exists. This view is called monistic materialism or physicalism or philosophical behaviourism. More recently this theory has also been called the 'identity theory', because it asserts that mental experiences are, in reality, identical with brain processes.

The various forms of monism will be replaced here by a pluralism: the thesis of the three worlds. This pluralism can be supported by two very different lines of argument. First, to show the reality of World 2 one can appeal to common sense, and to the failure of the physicalists to produce telling arguments against the commonsense view that a bad toothache can be very real indeed.

However, my second and main argument proceeds very differently. It starts from the assertion that World 3 objects, such as theories, do in fact strongly interact with the physical World 1. The simplest examples are the ways in which we make changes in World 1 when building, say, nuclear reactors or atom bombs or skyscrapers or airfields, in accordance with World 3 plans and with theories that are often highly abstract.

My main argument for the existence of the World 2 of subjective experiences is that we must normally grasp or understand a World 3 theory before we can use it to act upon World 1; but grasping or understanding a theory is a mental affair, a World 2 process: World 3 usually interacts with World 1 via the mental World 2. An example is the planning, construction, and use of bulldozers for the building of airfields. There is, first, an interaction between the World 2 planning by the human mind and the internal restrictions of both World 1 and World 3 which

[3] See *The Self and Its Brain*, Chapters P3 and P5.

117

limit the planning of the machinery. Secondly, we have an interaction between World 2 and the World 1 of the human brain, which in turn acts upon our limbs which steer the bulldozers.

The effectiveness of this argument clearly depends on World 3. If World 3 exists and is at least in part autonomous, and if, further, plans in World 3 do affect World 1, then it seems to me inescapable that there also exists a World 2. In this way my main argument for the existence of World 2 has led us back to the problem of whether World 3 exists; and further to the problem of whether World 3 is, in part, autonomous.

The Reality and Partial Autonomy of World 3

Human language and human thought evolve together, in mutual interaction. Human language, admittedly, expresses human thought processes, that is, World 2 objects. But it makes a very great difference to these subjective World 2 objects when they are formulated in an objective human language: there is a powerful feedback effect between human language and the human mind.

This is mainly because a thought, once it is formulated in language, becomes an *object* outside ourselves. Such an object can then be inter-subjectively *criticized*—criticized by others as well as by ourselves. Intersubjective or objective criticism in this sense only emerges with human language; and with it emerges the human World 3, the world of objective standards and of the contents of our subjective thought processes.

Thus it makes a great difference whether we merely *think* some thought or whether we *formulate* it in a language (or still better, write it down, or get it printed). As long as we merely think the thought it cannot be objectively criticized. It is part of ourselves. To be criticizable it must be formulated in a human language, and become an object: a World 3 object. Linguistically formulated thoughts belong to World 3. They can be *logically* criticized, for example by showing that they have certain unwelcome or even absurd logical consequences. Only *thought contents* belonging to

118

World 3 can stand in logical relationships, such as equivalence, deducibility, or contradiction.

Thus we must clearly distinguish between the subjective *thought processes,* which belong to World 2, and the objective *contents* of thoughts, the contents in themselves, as it were, which constitute World 3.

In order to make the point quite clear, take two mathematicians who, by making some mistakes, both arrive at a false theorem—for example, at the theorem that $5 + 7 = 13$. Their thought processes, which belong to World 2, can either be similar or entirely different. But the *content* of their thoughts, which belongs to World 3, is one and the same, and can be criticized. The two mathematicians can be kicked back by the logical structure of World 3, which shows that their alleged theorem *contradicts* the objectively *true* statement '$5 + 7 = 12$', and that it therefore must be objectively *false.* The two mathematicians are kicked; not by other people, but by the laws of arithmetic itself.

Most people are dualists: it is part of common sense to believe in the Worlds 1 and 2. But it is not easy for most people to accept the existence of World 3. They will of course admit that a very special part of World 1 exists which consists of printed books, or of acoustical language noises; and they will admit brain processes, and subjective thought processes. But they will assert that what distinguishes books from other physical bodies like trees, or human language from other noises like the howling of wolves, is *only* the fact that they help us to have certain special kinds of World 2 experiences, namely thought processes of a special kind (perhaps running parallel with brain processes) which are correlated with just these books or these linguistic noises.

I regard this view as totally insufficient. I shall try to show that we ought to admit the existence of an autonomous part of World 3; a part which consists of objective *thought contents* which are *independent of,* and clearly distinct from, the subjective or personal *thought processes* by which they are grasped, and whose grasp they can causally influence. I thus assert that there exist autonomous World 3 objects which have not yet taken up either World 1 shape or World 2 shape, but which, nevertheless,

119

interact with our thought processes. In fact, they influence our thought processes decisively.

Let us take an example from elementary arithmetic. The infinite sequence of natural numbers, 0, 1, 2, 3, 4, 5, 6, and so on, is a human invention, a product of the human mind. As such it may be said *not* to be autonomous, but to depend on World 2 thought processes. But now take the even numbers, or the prime numbers. These are not invented by us, but *discovered* or found. We *discover* that the sequence of natural numbers consists of even numbers and of odd numbers and, whatever we may think about it, no thought process can alter this fact of World 3. The sequence of natural numbers is a result of our learning to count—that is, it is an invention within the human language. But it has its unalterable inner laws or restrictions or regularities which are the *unintended consequences* of the man-made sequence of natural numbers; that is, the unintended consequences of some product of the human mind.

The same may be said about the prime numbers. It was found that the higher you proceed in the sequence of natural numbers (say, first to the numbers from 100 to 200, and then from 1100 to 1200) the rarer becomes the occurrence of prime numbers: this is an *autonomous property* of World 3. Now this discovery leads us to a new autonomous problem in World 3; a problem that is discovered, as simply being there, like the prime numbers themselves. It is the following interesting problem: if we proceed to greater and greater numbers, to 10 million, for example, do the prime numbers die out in the end, or are there *always* new prime numbers to come, even if they become rarer and rarer? Or in the terminology of Euclid, does there exist one greatest prime number or is the sequence of prime numbers infinite, like the sequence of natural numbers itself?

This is an objective and autonomous problem: either there exists a greatest prime number, or the sequence of prime numbers goes on and on, to infinity. Euclid, who may even have discovered the problem, solved it. He showed that the assumption that there exists a greatest prime number leads to an absurdity.

Thus he gave a proof, an indirect proof, of the objective fact that no greatest prime number exists but that there is always a greater one: the sequence of prime numbers is infinite, just as is that of natural numbers. And this fact is an objective, autonomous, fact of World 3. It is a World 3 theorem, an autonomous World 3 object. We can discover it, we can prove it, but we can do nothing to alter it.

The discovery of prime numbers has led to many difficult problems, some of which have been solved, and many of which are still open. These problems are discovered by us in the new field which we have created, in the sequence of natural numbers. They are discovered as being there, independently of whether anybody has thought of them before. Thus we have constructions in mathematics which are the products of the human mind, and problems and theories which are the objective and perhaps never thought of consequences of these constructions. This shows that the world of mathematics contains an autonomous part: an autonomous part of World 3.

My next point is that this autonomous part of World 3 is 'real' in the sense that it can interact with World 2 and also, via World 2, with World 1. If some men or many men seek for a solution of an as yet unsolved mathematical problem, then they are all, possibly in many different ways, influenced by this problem. The success of their attempts to solve it will depend, at least partly, upon the existence or non-existence, in World 3, of a solution to the problem, and partly upon whether or not they are led by their thought processes to objectively true thought contents. This shows that the autonomous World 3 objects can have a strong causal influence upon World 2 processes. And if a newly discovered World 3 problem, with or without a solution, is published, then the causal influence extends even into World 1, by helping to set in motion the fingers of typesetters and even the wheels of printing machines.

For simple reasons such as these, I hold not only that World 3 is partly autonomous, but that its autonomous part is real, since it can act upon World 1, at least via World 2. The situation is fundamentally the same for every scientific discovery and every technical invention. In all these cases, World 3 problems and

121

theories play a major role. The problems may be discovered, and though the theories (which are, say, about World 1) may be products of the human mind, they are *not merely* our constructs; for their truth or falsity depends entirely upon their relation to World 1, a relation which, in all important cases, we cannot alter. Their truth or falsity depends both upon the inner structure of World 3 (especially language) and upon World 1, the latter of which, as I have suggested, is the very standard of reality.

The Human Situation and the Natural World

The origin of life may be, for all we know at present, a unique occurrence in the universe. We cannot explain it and it comes very near to what David Hume would have called, grudgingly, a miracle. The emergence of a World 2 of animal consciousness, of feelings of joy and of pain, seems to be a second such miracle.

It seems reasonable to regard the emergence of consciousness and previously that of life as two comparatively recent events in the evolution of the universe; as events which, like the beginning of the universe, are at present, and perhaps for ever, beyond our scientific understanding. This modest approach admits freely the existence of open problems, and thereby does not close the way to discovering more about them—about their character and perhaps even about the ways to a possible solution, or at least to a partial solution.

A third great miracle is the emergence of the human brain, and of the human mind and of human reason. This third miracle may be less far removed than the others from an explanation, at least in evolutionary terms. Man is an animal. He appears to stand much nearer to the other animals than these stand to inanimate matter. But this is not to belittle the gulf which separates the human brain from the animal brain, and human language from all other animal languages—from the dispositions which most higher animals possess to *express* their inner states and to *communicate* with other animals.

Man has created human language, with its *descriptive* function and the value of truth, and with its *argumentative* function and the value of the validity of arguments, thus transcending animal languages with their merely expressive and communicative functions.[4] With it man has created the objective World 3, something for which there are only fairly remote analogues in the animal kingdom. And with this, he has produced a new world of civilization, of learning, of non-genetic growth: of growth that is not transmitted by the genetic code; of growth which depends not so much on natural selection as on selection based upon rational criticism.

It is, therefore, to the role of human language and of World 3 that we should look when we are trying to explain this third great miracle: the emergence of the human brain and of the human mind; of human reason and of human freedom.

Determinism and Indeterminism in Physics

The title of this essay is 'Indeterminism is Not Enough'; that is, not enough for human freedom. But I have yet to give at least a sketch of classical determinism (or physical determinism, or World 1 determinism), and of that indeterminism which is its opposite. Moreover, I have yet to show why these two ideas are insufficient for a discussion of human freedom.

Classical determinism, or World 1 determinism, is a very old idea which was most sharply formulated by Laplace, on the basis of Newton's mechanics. [See Section 10 above.]

Laplace's thesis of determinism can be stated in the following way. Assume we are given the exact masses, positions, and velocities of all material particles in the universe at some moment of time; then we can in principle calculate, with the help of Newtonian mechanics, all that has ever happened in the past and all that will ever happen in the future. This would include all the

---

[4] [For Popper's account of the functions of language, see his discussions in *Conjectures and Refutations*, Chapters 4, 12; *Objective Knowledge*, Chapters 2, 3, 4, 6; *Unended Quest*, section 15; and *The Self and Its Brain*, section 17, with particular reference to his discussion and amplification of Bühler's account. Ed.]

physical movements of all men, and therefore all spoken or written words, all poetry, and all the music that will ever be written. The calculation can be done by a machine. It need *only* be programmed with Newton's laws of motion and the existing initial conditions. It can be stone deaf, and unaware of the problems of musical composition. But it will be able to predict what black marks would be placed on white music paper by any given composer in the past or in the future.

I personally find Laplacean determinism a most unconvincing and unattractive view; and it is a doubtful argument, for the calculator may have greatly to exceed the universe in complexity, as was pointed out (first, I think) by F. A. Hayek.[5] But it is, perhaps, worth stressing that Laplace does draw the correct conclusions from his idea of a causally closed and deterministic World 1. If we accept Laplace's view, then we must not argue (as many philosophers do) that we are nevertheless endowed with genuine human freedom and creativity.

However, Laplacean determinism had to be modified upon the collapse of some attempts of Maxwell's to reduce electricity and magnetism to Newtonian mechanics by a mechanical model of the ether. With these attempts collapsed also the thesis of the closedness of Newton's mechanical World 1: it became open towards the electromagnetic part of World 1. Nevertheless, Einstein, for example, remained a determinist. He believed, almost to the end of his life, that a unified and closed deterministic theory was possible, comprising mechanics, gravitation, and electricity. In fact, most physicists are inclined to regard a causally open (and therefore indeterministic) physical universe—say, a physical universe that is open to the influence of World 2—as a typical superstition, upheld only perhaps by some spiritualist members of the Society for Psychical Research. Few physicists of repute would take it seriously.

But another form of indeterminism became part of the official creed of physics. The new indeterminism was introduced by quantum mechanics, which assumes the possibility of elementary chance events that are causally irreducible.

[5] F. A. von Hayek: *The Sensory Order*, 1952, Chapter 8, section 6.

There are, it appears, two kinds of chance events. One kind is due to the independence of two causal chains which happen, accidentally, to interfere at some place and time, and so combine in bringing about the chance event. A typical example consists of two causal chains, one of which loosens a brick while the other independent causal chain makes a man take up a position where he will be hit by the brick. This kind of chance event (whose theory was developed by Laplace himself, in his work on probability) is perfectly compatible with Laplacean determinism: anybody furnished in advance with sufficiently full information about the relevant events could have predicted what was bound to happen. It was only *the incompleteness of our knowledge* which gave rise to this kind of chance.

Quantum mechanics, however, introduced chance events of a second, and much more radical kind: absolute chance. According to quantum mechanics, there are elementary physical processes which are not further analyzable in terms of causal chains, but which consist of so-called 'quantum jumps'; and a quantum jump is supposed to be an absolutely unpredictable event which is controlled neither by causal laws nor by the coincidence of causal laws, but by probabilistic laws alone.[6] Thus quantum mechanics introduced, in spite of the protests of Einstein, what he described as 'the dice-playing God'. Quantum mechanics regards these absolute chance events as the basic events of World 1. The various particular results of these chance events, such as the disintegration of an atom with consequent radioactive emission, are not predetermined and therefore cannot be predicted however great our knowledge of all relevant conditions prior to the event may be. But we can make testable statistical predictions about such processes.

Although I do not believe that quantum mechanics will remain

---

[6] [Popper may seem at this place to concede that there are quantum jumps while elsewhere agreeing with Schrödinger that there are not (see *Quantum Theory and the Schism in Physics*, Vol. III of this *Postscript*, section 13). Questioned about this, he said that, while upholding the impossibility of predicting the jumps other than probabilistically, he agrees with Schrödinger that it is an open problem whether we must adopt an interpretation of the formalism that makes the quantum jumps instantaneous. Ed.]

the last word in physics, I happen to believe that its indeterminism is fundamentally sound. I believe that even classical Newtonian mechanics is in principle indeterministic. This becomes clear if we introduce into it physical models of human knowledge—for example, computers.[7] The introduction of objective human knowledge into our universe—the introduction of a World 3 (we must not forget that computers, even though inhuman, are man-made)—allows us to prove not only the indeterministic character of this universe, but its essential openness or incompleteness.

Returning now to quantum mechanics, I want to point out that the indeterminism of a dice-playing God, or of probabilistic laws, fails to make room for human freedom. For what we want to understand is not only how we may act *unpredictably and in a chancelike fashion,* but how we can act *deliberately and rationally.* The famous probabilistic constancy of such chance events as the posting of letters bearing no address may be an interesting curiosity, but it has no similarity whatever to the problem of the freedom to write a piece of poetry, good or bad, or to advance a new hypothesis concerning, say, the origin of the genetic code.

It must be admitted that if quantum mechanics is right, then Laplacean determinism is wrong and that arguments from physics can no longer be used to combat the doctrine of indeterminism. But indeterminism is not enough.

Indeterminism Is Not Enough

Let us take the physical world to be *partially* but not completely determined. That is to say, let us assume that events follow each other according to physical laws, but that there is sometimes a certain *looseness* in their connection, filled in by unpredictable and perhaps probabilistic sequences similar to

[7] [See Popper's discussions in *The Poverty of Historicism,* Preface; 'Indeterminism in Quantum Physics and in Classical Physics', *British Journal for the Philosophy of Science* 1, No. 2, pp. 117–133, and No. 3, pp. 173–195; and sections 20–22 of this volume of the *Postscript.* Ed.]

those we know from roulette or from dicing or from tossing a coin or from quantum mechanics. Thus we would have an indeterministic World 1, as indeed I have suggested that we have. *But nothing is gained for us if this World 1 is causally closed towards World 2 and World 3.* Such an indeterministic World 1 would be unpredictable; yet World 2, and with it World 3, could not have any influence upon it. A *closed* indeterministic World 1 would go on as before, whatever our feelings or wishes are, with the sole difference from Laplace's world that we could not predict it, even if we knew *all* about its present state: it would be a world ruled, if only partly, by chance.

Thus indeterminism is *necessary but insufficient* to allow for human freedom and especially for creativity. What we really need is the thesis that *World 1 is incomplete;* that it can be influenced by World 2; that it can interact with World 2; or that it is causally *open* towards World 2, and hence, further, towards World 3.

We thus come back to our central point: we must demand that World 1 is not self-contained or 'closed', but open towards World 2; that it can be influenced by World 2, just as World 2 can be influenced by World 3 and, of course, also by World 1.

Determinism and Naturalism

There can be little doubt that the fundamental philosophical motive in favour of a Laplacean determinism and the theory that World 1 is causally closed is the realization that man is an animal, and the wish to see ourselves as part of nature. I believe that the motive is right; if nature were fully deterministic then so would be the realm of human actions; in fact there would be no actions, but at most the appearance of actions.

But the argument can be turned around. If man is free, at least in part free, then so is nature; and the physical World 1 is open. And there is every reason to regard man as at least partly free. The opposite view—that of Laplace—leads to predestination. It leads to the view that billions of years ago, the elementary particles of World 1 contained the poetry of Homer, the philosophy of Plato, and the symphonies of Beethoven as a seed contains a plant; that human history is predestined, and with it all acts of human creativity. And the quantum theoretical version of the view is just as bad. If it has any bearing on human creativity, then it makes human creativity a matter of sheer chance. No doubt there is an element of chance in it. *Yet the theory that the creation of works of art or music can, in the last instance, be explained in terms of chemistry or physics seems to me absurd.* So far as the creation of music can be explained, it has to be explained at least partly in terms of the influence of other music (which also stimulates the creativity of the musician); and, most important, in terms of the inner structure, the internal laws and restrictions, which play such a role in music and in all other World 3 phenomena—laws and restrictions whose absorption (and whose occasional defiance) are immensely important for the musician's creativity.

Thus our freedom and especially our freedom to create stand, clearly, under the restrictions of all three worlds. Had Beethoven, by some misfortune, been deaf from birth, he would hardly have become a composer. As a composer he freely subordinated his freedom to the structural restrictions of World 3. The autonomous World 3 was the world in which he made his great and genuine discoveries, being free to choose his path like a discoverer in the Himalayas, but being restrained by the path so far chosen and by the restrictions of the world he was discovering. (Similar remarks could be made about Gödel.)

The Open Universe

Thus we are led back to assert that there is interaction between the Worlds 1, 2, and 3.

There is no doubt in my mind that Worlds 2 and 3 do interact. If we try to grasp or understand a theory, or to remember a symphony, then our minds are causally influenced; not merely by the memory of noises stored in our brains, but at least in part by the work of the composer, by the autonomous inner structures of the World 3 object which we try to grasp.

All this means that World 3 can act upon the World 2 of our minds. But if so, there is no doubt that, when a mathematician *writes down* his World 3 results on (physical) paper, his mind—his World 2—acts upon the physical World 1. Thus World 1 is open towards World 2, just as World 2 is open towards World 3.

This is of fundamental importance; for it shows that nature, or the universe to which we belong, and which contains as parts the Worlds 1, 2, and 3, is itself open; it contains World 3, and World 3 can be shown to be *intrinsically open*.

One aspect of the openness of World 3 is a consequence of Gödel's theorem that axiomatized arithmetic is not completable. Yet the incompletability and openness of the universe is perhaps best illustrated by a version of the well-known story of the man who draws a map of his room, including in his map the map which he is drawing. His task defies completion, for he has to take account, within his map, of his latest entry.

The story of the map is a trivial case compared with World 3 theories and their impact upon World 1, although it illustrates in a simple way the incompleteness of a universe that contains World 3 objects of knowledge. But so far it does not yet illustrate indeterminism. For each of the different 'last' strokes actually entered into the map determines, within the infinite sequence of entries to be made, a determined entry. However, this determinacy of the strokes holds only if we do not consider the fallibility of all human knowledge (a fallibility which plays a considerable role in the problems, theories and mistakes of World 3). Taking this into account, each of these 'last' strokes entered into our map constitutes for the draughtsman a new *problem*, the problem of entering a *further* stroke which depicts the 'last' stroke *precisely*. Because of the fallibility that characterizes all human knowledge, this problem cannot possibly be solved by the draughtsman with absolute precision; and the smaller the strokes to which the draughtsman proceeds, the greater will be the relative imprecision which will in principle be unpredictable and indeterminate, and which will constantly increase. In this way, the story of the map shows how the fallibility which affects objective human knowledge contributes to the essential indeterminism and openness of a universe that contains human knowledge as a part of itself.

The universe is thus bound to be open if it contains human

knowledge; papers, and books, like the present one, which are on the one hand physical World 1 objects, and, on the other, World 3 objects that fallibly try to state or to describe fallible human knowledge.

Thus we live in an open universe. We could not make this discovery before there was human knowledge. But once we have made it there is no reason to think that the openness depends exclusively upon the existence of human knowledge. It is much more reasonable to reject all views of a closed universe—that of a causally as well as that of a probabilistically closed universe; thus rejecting the closed universe envisaged by Laplace, as well as the one envisaged by wave mechanics. Our universe is partly causal, partly probabilistic, and partly open: it is emergent. The opposite view results from mistaking the character of our man-made World 3 theories about World 1—especially their characteristic oversimplifications—for the character of World 1 itself. We might have known better.

No good reason has been offered so far against the openness of our universe, or against the fact that radically new things are constantly emerging from it; and no good reasons have been offered so far that shed doubt upon human freedom and creativity, a creativity which is restricted as well as inspired by the inner structure of World 3.

Man is certainly part of nature, but, in creating World 3, he has transcended himself *and* nature, as it existed before him. And human freedom is indeed part of nature, but it transcends nature—at least as it existed before the emergence of human language and of critical thought, and of human knowledge.

Indeterminism is not enough: to understand human freedom we need more; we need the openness of World 1 towards World 2, and of World 2 towards World 3, and the autonomous and intrinsic openness of World 3, the world of the products of the human mind and, especially, of human knowledge.

SCIENTIFIC REDUCTION AND THE ESSENTIAL INCOMPLETENESS OF ALL SCIENCE[1]

I

Determinism is, historically, very closely connected with the thesis of 'reductionism'. A 'scientific' determinist, in the sense presented in this book, must be a reductionist; although it is not necessary for a reductionist to be a determinist. In this Addendum, I wish to discuss reductionism briefly.

The outstanding questions of reduction are, I believe, three:

(1) Can we reduce, or hope to reduce, biology to physics, or to physics and chemistry?

(2) Can we reduce to biology, or hope to reduce to biology, those subjective conscious experiences which we may ascribe to animals and, if question (1) is answered in the affirmative, can we reduce them further to physics and chemistry?

(3) Can we reduce, or hope to reduce, the consciousness of self and the creativeness of the human mind to animal experience, and thus, if questions (1) and (2) are answered in the affirmative, to physics and chemistry?

Obviously the replies to these three questions (to which I shall turn later) will partly depend on the meaning of the word 'reduce'. But for reasons which I have given elsewhere, I am opposed to the method of meaning analysis and to the attempt to solve serious problems by definitions. What I propose to do instead is this.

[1] [This Addendum was not part of the original *Postscript,* and is a revised version of an essay originally published in F. J. Ayala and T. Dobzhansky, eds.: *Studies in the Philosophy of Biology,* 1974. Ed.]

I will begin by discussing some examples of successful and unsuccessful reductions in the various sciences, and especially the reduction of chemistry to physics; and also the residues left by these reductionist research progammes.

In the course of this discussion, I will defend three theses. First, I will suggest that scientists have to be reductionists in the sense that nothing is as great a success in science as a successful reduction (such as Newton's reduction to—or rather explanation by[2]—his theory of Kepler's and Galileo's laws, and his correction of them). A successful reduction is, perhaps, the most successful form conceivable of all scientific explanations, since it achieves what Meyerson stressed: an *identification* of the unknown with the known.[3] By contrast with a reduction, however, an explanation with the help of a new theory explains the known—the known problem—by something unknown: by a new conjecture.[4]

Secondly, I will suggest that scientists *have* to welcome reductionism as a *method*: they have to be either naïve or else more or less critical reductionists; indeed, somewhat desperate critical reductionists, I shall argue, because hardly any major reduction in science has ever been *completely* successful: there is almost always an unresolved residue left by even the most successful reductionist research programmes.

Thirdly, I shall contend that there do not seem to be any good arguments in favour of *philosophical* reductionism, while, on the contrary, there are good arguments against essentialism, with which philosophical reductionism seems to be closely allied.[5] We

[2] [See *Objective Knowledge*, Chapter 5; and *Realism and the Aim of Science* (Vol. I of the *Postscript*), section 15. Ed.]

[3] E. Meyerson: *Identity and Reality*, 1908, English translation 1930.

[4] See *Conjectures and Refutations*, pp. 63, 102, 174.

[5] I disregard here—perhaps carelessly, or because I dislike terminological minutiae—the distinction that can well be made between explanation in general, and 'reduction' in the sense of an explanation by way of a better tested or more 'fundamental' theory. A distinction of major interest, I suppose, would be that between an explanation of something known by a new (unknown) theory, on one hand, and a reduction to an old (known) theory on the other. A distinction could I suppose be made between a *reduction* which explains some theory by an existing theory and an *explanation with the help of a new theory*: though I will not quarrel about words I should be disinclined to call an explanation with the

should, nevertheless, on methodological grounds, continue to attempt reductions. For we can learn an immense amount even from unsuccessful or incomplete attempts at reduction, and problems left open in this way belong to our most valuable intellectual possessions: a greater emphasis upon what are often regarded as our scientific failures (or, in other words, upon the great open problems of science) can do us a lot of good.

II

Apart from Newton's, one of the few reductions known to me which have been almost completely successful is the reduction of rational fractions to ordered pairs of natural numbers (that is, to relations or ratios between them). Although it was achieved by the Greeks, one might say that even this reduction left a *residue* which was dealt with only in the twentieth century (with the successful reduction, by Wiener (1914) and Kuratowski (1920), of the ordered pair to an unordered pair of unordered pairs; moreover, one should be aware that the reduction is one to *sets* of equivalent pairs, rather than to pairs themselves). It encouraged the Pythagorean cosmological research programme[6] of arithmetization, which, however, broke down with the proof of the existence of irrationals such as the square roots of 2, 3, or 5.[7] Plato replaced the cosmological research programme of arithmetization by one of geometrization, and this programme

help of a new theory a 'reduction'. Yet if this terminology is adopted the explanation of the wave theory of the propagation of light by Maxwell's theory of electromagnetism could be claimed as an example of a completely successful reduction (perhaps the only example of a completely successful reduction). However, it may be better not to describe this as a reduction of one theory to another, or one part of physics to another, but rather as a radically new theory which succeeded in unifying two parts of physics.

[For Popper's discussion of essentialism in this context, and for the connection of that with justificationism, see *Realism and the Aim of Science* (Vol. I of the *Postscript*), section 2; see also *Unended Quest*, section 7, and *The Open Society*, Chapter 11. Ed.]

[6] [For Popper's idea of research programmes, see *Quantum Theory and the Schism in Physics* (Vol. III of the *Postscript*), Metaphysical Epilogue. Ed.]

[7] See *The Open Society and Its Enemies*, Vol. I, Chapter 6, *n.* 9; and *Conjectures and Refutations*, Chapter 2, pp. 75–92.

was carried on successfully from Euclid to Einstein. However, the invention of the calculus by Newton and Leibniz (and the problem of excluding some paradoxical results which their own intuitive methods failed to exclude) created the need for a new arithmetization—a new reduction to natural numbers. In spite of the most spectacular successes of the nineteenth and early twentieth centuries, this reduction has not been fully successful.

To mention only one unresolved residue, a reduction to a sequence of natural numbers or to a set in the sense of modern set theory is not the same as, or even similar to, a reduction to a set of equivalent ordered pairs of natural numbers. As long as the idea of a set was used naïvely and purely intuitively (as by Cantor) this was perhaps not obvious. But the paradoxes of infinite sets (discussed by Bolzano, Cantor and Russell) and the need to axiomatize set theory showed, to say the very least, that the reduction achieved was not a straightforward arithmetization—a reduction to natural numbers—but a reduction to axiomatic set theory; and this turned out to be a highly sophisticated and somewhat perilous enterprise.

To sum up this example, the programme of arithmetization— that is, of the reduction of geometry and the irrationals to natural numbers—has partly failed. But the number of unexpected problems and the amount of unexpected knowledge brought about by this failure are overwhelming. This may be generalized: even where we do not succeed as reductionists, the number of interesting and unexpected results we may acquire on the way to our failure can be of the greatest value.

III

I have mentioned the partial failure of the attempted reduction of the irrationals to natural numbers, and I have also indicated that programmes of reduction are part of the activities of scientific and mathematical explanation, simplification and understanding.

I will now discuss in a little more detail some successes and failures of programmes of reduction in physics, and in particular the partial successes of the reduction of macrophysics to microphysics and of chemistry to both microphysics and macro-physics.

I use the name 'ultimate explanation' for the attempt to explain or reduce things by an appeal to something that is neither in need of, nor capable of, further explanation, more especially an 'essence' or a 'substance' *(ousia)*. [8]

A striking example is the Cartesian reduction of the whole of the physics of inanimate bodies to *extended substance*; a sub-stance (matter) with only one essential property; that is, spatial extension. [9]

This attempt to reduce the whole of physics to the one apparently essential property of matter was highly successful in so far as it gave rise to an understandable picture of the physical universe. The Cartesian physical universe was a moving clockwork of vortices in which each 'body' or 'part of matter' pushed its neighbouring part along, and was pushed along by its neighbour on the other side. Matter alone was to be found in the physical world, and all space was filled by it. In fact, space too was reduced to matter, since there was no empty space but only the essential spatial extension of matter. And there was only one purely physical mode of causation: *all causation was push,* or action by contact.

This way of looking at the world was found satisfactory even by Newton, though he felt compelled to introduce by his theory of gravity a new kind of causation: *attraction,* or action at a distance.

The almost incredible explanatory and predictive success of Newton's theory destroyed the Cartesian reduction programme. Newton himself attempted to carry out the Cartesian reduction programme by explaining gravitational attraction by the 'impulse' (radiation pressure combined with an umbrella effect) of a cosmic particle bombardment (the attempt is usually linked with the name of LeSage). [10] But I believe that Newton became aware

[8] See *Conjectures and Refutations*, Chapter 3, pp. 103–7.

[9] See *The Self and Its Brain*, Chapters P1 and P3; and *Quantum Theory and the Schism in Physics* (Vol. III of the *Postscript*), Metaphysical Epilogue.

[10] See *Conjectures and Refutations*, p. 107, note 21.

of the fatal objection to this theory. Admittedly it would reduce attraction and action at a distance to push and to action by contact; but it would also mean that all moving bodies would move in a resisting medium which would act as a brake on their movement (consider the excess push of rain on the windscreen of a car over that on the rear window) and which would thus invalidate Newton's use of the law of inertia.

Thus, in spite of its intuitive attractiveness, and in spite of Newton's own rejection as 'absurd' of the view that attraction at a distance could be an essential property of matter, the attempt at an ultimate reduction of attraction to push breaks down.

We have here a simple example of a promising scientific reduction and its failure, and of how much one can learn by attempting a reduction and discovering that, and perhaps even why, it fails.

(I conjecture that this failure was the immediate reason why Newton described space as the sensorium of God. Space was 'aware', so to speak, of the distribution of all bodies: it was, in a sense, omniscient. It was also omnipresent, for it transmitted this knowledge with infinite velocity to all locations at every moment of time. Thus space, sharing at least two characteristic properties of the divine essence, was itself part of the divine essence. This, I suggest, was another attempt by Newton at an essentialist ultimate explanation.)

The Cartesian reduction illustrates why for methodological reasons we must attempt reductions. But it may also indicate why we must not be sanguine but can only be somewhat despairing concerning the complete success of our attempted reductions.

IV

The Cartesian attempt to reduce everything in the physical world to extension and push was a failure when compared with the success of Newton's own theory of gravity. That success was so great that Newtonians, beginning with Roger Cotes, began to look upon Newtonian theory itself as an ultimate explanation and thus at *gravitational attraction* as an essential property of matter, in spite of Newton's own views to the contrary. But Newton had seen no reason why *extension* (of his atoms) and *inertia* should not be essential properties of mass.[11] Thus Newton was clearly aware of the distinction, later stressed by Einstein, between inertial and gravitational mass, and of the problem opened by their proportionality (or equality); a problem which, because of the obscurantism of the essentialist approach, was almost lost sight of between Newton and Eötvös or even Einstein.

Einstein's special relativity theory destroyed the essentialist identity of inertial and gravitational mass, and this is why he tried to explain it, somewhat *ad hoc*, by his principle of equivalence. But when it was discovered (first by Cornelius Lanczos) that Einstein's equations of gravitation led by themselves to the principle, previously separately assumed, that gravitating bodies move on a space-time geodesic, the principle of inertia was in fact reduced to the equations of gravitation and thus inertial mass to gravitational mass. (I believe that Einstein, though strongly impressed by the importance of this result, did not fully accept that it solved Mach's central problem—the explanation of inertia—in a more satisfactory way than the famous but far from unambiguous 'Mach principle': the principle that the inertia of each body is due to the combined effect of all the other bodies in the universe. To Einstein's disappointment, this principle was, at least in some of its interpretations, incompatible with general relativity which, for a space empty of all bodies, yields special relativity, in which the law of inertia, contrary to Mach's suggestion, is still valid.)

Here we have a most satisfying example of a successful reduction: the reduction of a generalized principle of inertia to a generalized principle of gravitation. But it has been rarely considered in this light; not even by Einstein, though he strongly felt the significance of a result which, from a purely mathematical point of view, could be regarded as elegant but not particularly important. For the dependence or independence of an axiom within a system of axioms is in general not of more than formal

[11] See *Conjectures and Refutations*, pp. 106 *ff.*

interest. Why should it matter, therefore, whether the law of motion on a geodesic had to be assumed as a separate axiom or could be derived from the rest of gravitational theory? The answer is that by its derivation, the identity of inertial and gravitational mass was *explained,* and the former reduced to the latter.

In this way one might say that Newton's great problem of action at a distance (couched in the phraseology of essentialism) was solved not so much by the finite velocity of Einsteinian gravitational action as by the reduction of inertial matter to gravitational matter.

V

Newton and the Newtonians knew, of course, about the existence of magnetic and electrical forces; and until at least the beginning of the twentieth century, attempts were made to reduce electromagnetic theory to Newtonian mechanics, or to a modified form of it.

The outstanding problem in this development was the reduction of *prima facie* non-central forces (Oersted forces) to central forces, the only ones which seemed to fit into even a modified Newtonian theory. The outstanding names in this development were Ampère and Weber.

Maxwell too began by trying to reduce Faraday's electromagnetic field of (lines of) forces to a Newtonian mechanism or model of the luminiferous ether. But he gave up the attempt (though not the luminiferous ether as the carrier of the electromagnetic field). Helmholtz also was attracted by a Newtonian and partly Cartesian reduction programme, and when he suggested to his pupil, Heinrich Hertz, that he should work on this problem, Helmholtz seems to have done so in the hope of saving the research programme of mechanics. But he accepted Hertz's confirmation of Maxwell's equations as crucial. After Hertz and J. J. Thomson, precisely the opposite research programme became more attractive—the programme of reducing mechanics to electromagnetic theory.

The electromagnetic theory of matter—that is, the reduction of both mechanics and chemistry to an electromagnetic theory of atomism—was strikingly successful from at least 1912, the year of Rutherford's planetary or nuclear atom model, until about 1932.

In fact, quantum mechanics (or 'the new quantum theory', as it was once called) was, until at least 1935, simply another name for what was then regarded as the final form of the reduction of mechanics to the new *electromagnetic theory of matter*.

In order to realize how important this reduction appeared to leading physicists even shortly before quantum mechanics, I may quote Einstein who wrote:[12]

> . . . according to our present conceptions the elementary particles [that is, electrons and protons] are . . . *nothing else* than condensations of the electromagnetic field . . . , our . . . view of the universe presents two realities . . . , namely, gravitational ether and electromagnetic field, or—as they might also be called—space and matter.

The 'nothing else' which I have italicized is characteristic of reduction in the grand style. Indeed, to the end of his life, Einstein tried to unify the gravitational and the electromagnetic fields in a unified field theory, even after his view of 1920 had been superseded—or rather, had broken down (especially owing to the discovery of nuclear forces).

What amounts, essentially, to the same reductionist view was accepted at that time (1932) by almost all leading physicists: Eddington and Dirac in England and, besides Einstein, Bohr, de Broglie, Schrödinger, Heisenberg, Born and Pauli on the continent of Europe. And a very impressive statement of the view was given by Robert A. Millikan, then of the California Institute of Technology:[13]

---

[12] A. Einstein: *Äther und Relativitätstheorie*, 1922, translated as *Sidelights on Relativity*, 1922, p. 24. See also my 'Quantum Mechanics without "the Observer" ', in Mario Bunge, ed.: *Quantum Theory and Reality*, 1967, pp. 7–44, now reprinted in revised version as the Introduction to *Quantum Theory and the Schism in Physics* (Vol. III of the *Postscript*).

[13] R. A. Millikan: *Time, Matter and Values*, 1932, p. 46.

Indeed, nothing more beautifully simplifying has ever happened in the history of science than the whole series of discoveries culminating about 1914 which finally brought practically universal acceptance to the theory that the material world contains but two fundamental entities, namely, positive and negative electrons, exactly alike in charge, but differing widely in mass, the positive electron—now usually called a proton—being 1850 times heavier than the negative, now usually called simply the electron.

This reductionist passage was written in the very nick of time: it was in the same year (1932) that Chadwick published his discovery of the neutron, and that Anderson first discovered the positron. Yet some of the greatest physicists, such as Eddington (1936), continued to believe, even after Yukawa's suggestion of the existence of what was to be called the meson (1935), that with the advent of quantum mechanics the electromagnetic theory of matter had entered into its final state and that all matter consisted of electrons and protons.[14]

Indeed, the reduction of mechanics and of chemistry to the electromagnetic theory of matter seemed almost perfect. What had appeared to Descartes and Newton as the space-filling essence of matter, and as Cartesian push, had been reduced (as Leibniz had demanded long ago) to *repulsive forces*—the forces exerted by negative electrons upon negative electrons. The electrical neutrality of matter was explained by the equal number of positive protons and negative electrons; and the electrification (ionization) of matter was explained by a loss of electrons from (or excess of electrons in) the planetary electron shell of the atom.

Chemistry had been reduced to physics (or so it seemed) by Bohr's quantum theory of the periodic system of elements, a theory which was ingeniously perfected by the use of Pauli's exclusion principle; and the theory of chemical composition, and of the nature of covalent chemical bonds, was reduced by Heitler

[14] J. Chadwick: 'Possible existence of a neutron', *Nature* **129**, p. 132; C. D. Anderson: 'Cosmic ray bursts', *Physical Review* **43**, pp. 368–9, and 'The positive electron', *Physical Review* **43**, pp. 491–4; A. Eddington: *Relativity Theory of Protons and Electrons*, 1936; and H. Yukawa: 'On the interaction of elementary particles', *Proceedings of the Physico-Mathematical Society of Japan*, 3rd. series, **17**, pp. 48–57.

and London (1927) to a theory of (homeopolar) valency which again made use of Pauli's principle.

Although matter was revealed to be a complex structure rather than an irreducible substance, there had never before been such unity in the universe of physics, or such a degree of reduction.

Nor has it ever been achieved again since.

True, we still believe in the reduction of Cartesian push to electromagnetic forces; and Bohr's theory of the periodic system of elements, though considerably changed by the introduction of isotopes, has largely survived. But everything else in this beautiful reduction of the universe to an electromagnetic universe with two particles as stable building blocks has by now disintegrated. Emphatically, we have learned an immense number of new facts in the process of this disintegration: this is one of my main theses. *But the simplicity, and the reduction programme, have gone.*

This process, which started with the discovery of neutrons and of positrons, has continued with the discovery of new elementary particles ever since. But particle theory is not even the main difficulty. The real disruption is due to the discovery of new kinds of forces, especially of short-range nuclear forces, apparently irreducible to electromagnetic and gravitational forces.

Gravitational forces did not trouble the physicists very much in those days, because they had just been explained away by general relativity, and it was hoped that the dualism of gravitational and electromagnetic forces would be superseded by a unified field theory. But now we have at least four very different and still irreducible kinds of forces in physics: gravitation, weak decay interaction, electromagnetic forces and nuclear forces.[15]

---

[15] Today there are new, broader attempts to attain a unified field theory—attempts to unify all four natural forces. Among these, we may mention the work of Steven Weinberg and Abdus Salam, and what is often called the 'Weinberg-Salam Theory of Weak Interaction', or 'gauge theory'. This theory proposes that electromagnetic forces and weak nuclear forces (which cause radioactive decay in some kinds of atomic nuclei) are aspects or facets of the same phenomenon; and there has been some corroboration of this proposal through tests of neutral current in atomic nuclei. But gravitational and strong nuclear forces still lie beyond this theory, and the theory itself is thus in some respects still a metaphysical research programme.

VI

Thus Cartesian mechanics—once regarded by Descartes and Newton as the basis to which all else was to be reduced—was, and still is, successfully reduced to electromagnetism. But what about the admittedly most impressive reduction of chemistry to quantum physics?

Let us assume for argument's sake that we have a fully satisfactory reduction to the quantum theory of chemical bonds (both of covalent or twin electron bonds and of non-covalent, for example plug-and-hole, bonds), in spite of the telling remark of Pauling (1959), author of *The Nature of the Chemical Bond*, that he was unable to 'define' (or state precisely) what the nature of the chemical bond was. Let us further assume for argument's sake that we have a fully satisfactory theory of nuclear forces, of the periodic system of the elements and their isotopes, and especially of the stability and instability of the heavier nuclei. Does this constitute a fully satisfactory reduction of chemistry to quantum mechanics?

I do not think it does. An entirely new idea has to be brought in, an idea which is somewhat foreign to physical theory: the idea of evolution, of the history of our universe, of cosmogony, and even more of cosmogeny.

This is so because the periodic table of the elements and the (reformulated) Bohr theory of the periodic system explain the heavier nuclei as being composed of lighter ones; ultimately as being composed of hydrogen nuclei (protons) and neutrons (which in turn *might* be regarded as a kind of composition of protons and electrons). And this theory assumes that the heavier elements have a history—that the properties of their nuclei actually result from a rare process which makes several hydrogen nuclei fuse into heavier nuclei, under conditions which are only rarely encountered in the cosmos.

We have much evidence in favour of the view that this really happened and still happens; that the heavier elements have an evolutionary history and that the fusion process by which heavy hydrogen is transformed into helium is the main source of the energy of our own sun and also of the hydrogen bomb. Thus helium and all the heavier elements are the result of cosmological evolution. Their history, and especially the history of the heavier elements, is, according to present cosmological views, a strange one. The heavier elements are at present regarded as the products of supernovae explosions. Since helium, according to some recent estimates, forms twenty-five per cent of all matter by mass and hydrogen two-thirds or three-quarters of all matter by mass, all the heavier nuclei appear to be extremely rare (together perhaps one or two per cent by mass). Thus the earth and presumably the other planets of our solar system are made mainly of very rare (and I should say very precious) materials.

At present the most widely accepted theory of the origin of the universe[16]—that of the hot big bang—claims that most of the helium is the product of the big bang itself: that it was produced within the very first minute of the existence of the expanding universe. The precariousness of the scientific status of this speculation (originally due to Gamow) need not be stressed. And since we have to appeal to theories of this kind in our attempts to reduce chemistry to quantum mechanics, it can hardly be claimed that this reduction has been carried out without residue.

The truth is that we have reduced chemistry, at least in part, to cosmology rather than to physical theory. Admittedly, modern classical relativistic cosmology started as an applied physical theory; but, as Hermann Bondi says, these times seem now to be over, and we must face the fact that some of our ideas (for example, those that started with Dirac and Jordan) could almost be described as attempts to reduce physical theory to cosmogony. And both cosmology and cosmogony, though immensely fascinating parts of physics, and though they are becoming better testable, are still almost borderline cases of physical science, and hardly yet mature enough to serve as the bases of the reduction of chemistry to physics. This is one reason why I regard the so-called reduction of chemistry to physics as incomplete and

[16] This theory may now be threatened by the new theory of redshifts proposed by J. C. Pecker, A. P. Roberts and J.-P. Vigier, 'Non-velocity redshifts and photon-photon interactions', *Nature* 237, 1972, pp. 227–9.

somewhat problematic; although of course I greatly welcome all these new problems.

VII

But there is a second residue of the reduction of chemistry to physics. Our present view is that hydrogen alone, or rather its nucleus, is the building material of all the other nuclei. We believe that the positive nuclei strongly repel each other electrically down to very short distances, but that for still shorter distances (achievable only if the repulsion is overcome by tremendous pressures or velocities) they attract each other by nuclear forces.

But this means that we attribute to the hydrogen nucleus relational properties which are inoperative in the overwhelming majority of the conditions in which hydrogen nuclei exist in our universe. That is to say, these nuclear forces are potentialities that became active only late, under conditions which are extremely rare: under tremendous temperatures and pressures. But this means that the theory of the evolution of the periodic table looks very much like a theory of essential properties which have the character of *predestination, or of a pre-established harmony.* [17] At any rate, a solar system like ours depends, according to present theories, on the pre-existence of these properties, or rather, potentialities.

Moreover, the theory of the origin of the heavier elements in explosions of supernovae introduces *a second type of predestination or pre-established harmony.* For it amounts to the assertion that gravitational forces (apparently the weakest of all, and so far unconnected with nuclear or electromagnetic forces)[18] can, in big accumulations of hydrogen, become so powerful as to overcome the tremendous electrical repulsion between the nuclei, and to make them fuse due to the action of the nuclear forces. Here the harmony is between the inherent potentialities of nuclear forces

[17] I use the term 'pre-established harmony' here to stress that our explanation is not in terms of the manifest physical properties of the hydrogen atom. Rather, a hitherto unknown and unsuspected property of the hydrogen nucleus was postulated, and used as an explanation.

[18] See footnote 15 above.

and of gravitation. I do not want to say that a philosophy of pre-established harmony must be false. But I do not think that an appeal to pre-established harmony can be regarded as a satisfactory reduction; and I suggest that such an appeal is an admission of the failure of the method of reducing one thing to another.

Thus the reduction of chemistry to physics is far from complete, even if we admit somewhat unrealistically favourable assumptions. Rather, this reduction assumes a theory of cosmic evolution or cosmogeny, and in addition two kinds of pre-established harmony, in order to allow sleeping potentialities, or relative propensities of low probability built into the hydrogen atom, to become activated. It appears, I suggest, that we should recognize that we are operating with the ideas of *emergence* and of *emergent properties*. [19] In this way we see that this very interesting reduction has left us with a strange picture of the universe—strange, at any rate to the reductionist; which is the point I wanted to make in this section.

VIII

To sum up what has been said so far: I have tried to make the problem of reduction clear with the help of examples, and I have tried to show that some of the most impressive reductions in the

---

[19] I use here the term 'emergent' to indicate an apparently unforeseeable evolutionary step. See *The Self and Its Brain*, 1977, Chapter P1, sections 6–9. Without wishing to advocate what one might call an antireductionistic research programme for biology, the following seems to be a reasonable comment on the situation. The mechanistic research programme for physics broke down over the attempt to include electricity and magnetism, or, more precisely, over Faraday's introduction of non-central forces. (Maxwell's attempt to reduce these non-central forces to Newtonian theory by constructing a mechanical model of the ether proved extremely fruitful in suggesting to him his field equations, but nevertheless was unsuccessful and had to be dropped.) Einstein's realization that Newton's and Maxwell's theories do not fuse led to general relativity. So physicists had to accept a radically new theory rather than a reduction. A similar fate befell physics when both mechanics and electromagnetic theory in the unified form due to Lorentz and Einstein were applied to new and largely statistical problems of the microstructure of matter. This led to quantum mechanics. We cannot rule out the possibility that the inclusion of biological problems may lead to a further expansion and revision of physics.

history of the physical sciences are far from completely successful, and leave a residue. One might claim (but see footnote 5
above) that Newton's theory was a completely successful reduction of Kepler's and Galileo's. But even if we assume that we
know much more physics than we do, and that we have a unified
field theory that yields with high approximation general relativity, quantum theory and the four kinds of forces as special
cases, even then we can say that chemistry has not been reduced
without residue to physics. In fact the so-called reduction of
chemistry is to a physics that assumes evolution, cosmology and
cosmogeny, and the existence of emergent properties.

On the other hand, in our not fully successful attempts at
reduction, especially of chemistry to physics, we have learned an
incredible amount. New problems have given rise to new con-
jectural theories, and some of these, such as nuclear fusion, have
led not only to corroborating experiments, but to a new technology. Thus from the point of view of method, our reduction
programmes have led to great successes, even though it may be
said that the attempted reductions have, as such, usually failed.

IX

The story told here and the lesson drawn from it will hardly
strike a biologist as unexpected. In biology too, reductionism (in
the form of physicalism or materialism) has been extremely
successful, though not fully successful. But even where it has not
succeeded, it has led to new problems and to new solutions.

I might perhaps express my view as follows. As a philosophy,
reductionism is a failure. From the point of view of method, the
attempts at detailed reductions have led to one staggering success
after another, and its failures have also been most fruitful for
science.

It is perhaps understandable that some of those who have
achieved these scientific successes have not been struck by the
failure of the philosophy. Perhaps my analysis of the success and
of the failure of the attempt to reduce chemistry completely to

quantum physics may give them pause, and may make them look at the problem again.

X

The discussion so far may be regarded as an elaboration of a brief remark made by Jacques Monod in the Preface to his *Chance and Necessity*:[20]

> Nor can everything in chemistry be predicted or resolved by means of the quantum theory [or reduced to quantum theory] which, beyond any question, underlies all chemistry.

In the same book, Monod also puts forward a suggestion (not an assertion, to be sure) concerning the origin of life, which is very striking, and which we may consider from the point of view reached here. Monod's suggestion is that life emerged from inanimate matter by an extremely improbable combination of chance circumstances, and that this may not merely have been an event of low probability but of zero probability—in fact, a *unique* event.

This suggestion is experimentally testable (as Monod has pointed out, in discussion with Eccles). Should we succeed in producing life under certain well-defined experimental conditions, then the hypothesis of the uniqueness of the origin of life would be refuted. Thus the suggestion is a testable scientific hypothesis, even though it may not look like one at first sight.

What, besides, makes Monod's suggestion plausible? There is the fact of the uniqueness of the genetic code, but this could be, as Monod points out, the result of natural selection. What makes the origin of life and of the genetic code a disturbing riddle is this: the genetic code is without any biological function unless it is translated; that is, unless it leads to the synthesis of the proteins whose structure is laid down by the code. But, as Monod points out, the machinery by which the cell (at least the non-primitive cell which is the only one we know) translates the code 'consists

[20] *Chance and Necessity*, 1971, p. xii.

of at least fifty macromolecular components *which are themselves coded in DNA*'.[21] Thus the code cannot be translated except by using certain products of its translation. This constitutes a really baffling circle: a vicious circle, it seems, for any attempt to form a model, or a theory, of the genesis of the genetic code.

Thus we may be faced with the possibility that the origin of life (like the origin of the universe) becomes an impenetrable barrier to science, and a residue to all attempts to reduce biology to chemistry and physics. For even though Monod's suggestion of the uniqueness of life's origin is refutable—by attempts at reduction, to be sure—it would amount, if true, to a denial of any fully successful reduction. With this suggestion Monod, who is a reductionist for reasons of method, arrives at the position which, I believe, is the one forced upon us all in the light of our earlier discussion of the reduction of chemistry to physics. It is the position of a critical reductionist who continues with attempted reductions even if he despairs of any ultimate success. Yet it is in going forward with attempted reductions, as Monod stresses elsewhere in his book, rather than in any replacement of reductionist methods by 'holistic' ones, that our main hope lies—our hope of learning more about old problems, and of discovering new problems which, in turn, may lead to new solutions, to new discoveries.

I do not want to discuss holism in any detail here, but a few words may be needed. The use of holistic experimental methods (such as cell transplantation in embryos), though inspired by holistic thought, may well be claimed to be methodologically reductionist. Holistic theories are, on the other hand, trivially needed in the description of even an atom or a molecule, not to speak of an organism or of a gene population. There is no limit to the variety of possibly fruitful conjectures, whether holistic or not.[22] In view of my main thesis, doubt arises only about the

21 *Ibid.*, p. 143.

22 Before we can even attempt a reduction, we need as great and as detailed a knowledge as possible of whatever it may be that we are trying to reduce. Thus before we can attempt a reduction, we need to work on the level of the thing to be reduced (that is, the level of 'wholes'). See my *Objective Knowledge*, pp. 285–318, esp. 297.

character of experimental methods in biology: whether they are not all, more or less, of a reductionist character. (A similar situation arises, incidentally, as David Miller reminds me, with regard to deterministic and indeterministic theories. Though we must, as I have argued in the body of this volume, be metaphysical *indeterminists,* methodologically we should still search for deterministic or causal laws—except where the problems to be solved are themselves of a probabilistic character.)

Even if Monod's suggestion of the uniqueness of the origin of life should be refuted by the production of life from inanimate matter under clearly repeatable conditions, this would not amount to a complete reduction. I do not wish to argue *a priori* that a reduction is impossible; but we have produced life from life for a long time without understanding what we have been doing, and before we had even an inkling of molecular biology or the genetic code. Thus it is certainly possible that we may produce life from inanimate matter without a full physicochemical understanding of what we are actually doing; for example, how we managed to break the vicious circle inherent in the translation of the code.

At any rate we can say that the undreamt-of breakthrough of molecular biology has made the problem of the origin of life a greater riddle than it was before: we have acquired new and deeper problems.

XI

The attempt to reduce chemistry to physics thus demands the introduction of a theory of evolution into physics; that is, a recourse to the history of our cosmos. A theory of evolution is, it appears, even more indispensable in biology. And so is, in addition, the idea of purpose or teleology or (to use Mayr's term) of teleonomy, or the very similar idea of problem solving; an idea which is quite foreign to the subject matter of the non-biological sciences (even though the role played in these sciences by maxima and minima and by the calculus of variations has been regarded as remotely analogous).

149

It was of course Darwin's great achievement to show that it is possible to explain teleology in non-teleological or ordinary causal terms. Darwinism is the best explanation we have. At the moment there are no seriously competing hypotheses.[23]

Problems and problem solving seem to emerge together with life. Even though there is something like natural selection at work prior to the origin of life—for example, a selection of the more stable elements due to the radioactive disintegration of the less stable ones—we cannot say that, for atomic nuclei, survival is a 'problem' in any sense of this term. And the close analogy between crystals and micro-organisms and their molecular parts (organelles) breaks down here too. Crystals have no problems of growth or of propagation or of survival. But life is faced with the problems of survival from the very beginning. Indeed, we can describe life, if we like, as problem solving, and living organisms as the only problem solving complexes in the universe. (Computers are *instrumental in* problem solving but not, in this sense, problem solvers.)

This does not mean that we have to ascribe to all life a *consciousness* of the problems to be solved: even on the human level we constantly solve many problems, such as keeping our balance, without becoming aware of them.

XII

There can be little doubt that animals possess consciousness and that, at times, they can even be conscious of a problem. But the emergence of consciousness in the animal kingdom is perhaps as great a mystery as is the origin of life itself.

I do not want to say more about this than that panpsychism, or hylozoism, or the thesis that matter is, generally, endowed with consciousness (of a low degree), does not seem to me to help in the least. It is, if taken at all seriously, another theory of predestination, a pre-established harmony. (It was of course part of Leibniz's original form of his theory of pre-established

[23] See *Objective Knowledge*, Chapters 6 and 7.

harmony.) For in non-living matter, consciousness has no function at all; and if (with Leibniz, Diderot, Buffon, Haeckel and many others) we attribute consciousness to nonliving particles (monads, atoms) then we do so in the vain hope that it will help to explain the presence of those forms of consciousness which have some function in animals.

For there can be little doubt that consciousness in animals has some function, and can be looked on as if it were a bodily organ. We have to assume, difficult as this may be, that it is a product of evolution, of natural selection.

Although this remark might be a programme for a reduction, it is not yet a reduction, and the situation for the reductionist looks somewhat desperate; which explains why reductionists have either adopted the hypothesis of panpsychism or why, more recently, they have denied the existence of consciousness (the consciousness, say, of a toothache) altogether.

Though this behaviourist philosophy is quite fashionable at present, a theory of the nonexistence of consciousness cannot be taken any more seriously, I suggest, than a theory of the nonexistence of matter. Both theories 'solve' the problem of the relationship between body and mind. The solution is in both cases a radical simplification: it is the denial either of body or of mind. But in my opinion it is too cheap.[24] I shall say a little more about this second 'outstanding question' and especially about panpsychism below, in section XIV, where I criticize psychophysical parallelism.

XIII

Of the three 'outstanding questions of reduction' listed at the beginning of this paper I have briefly touched upon two. I am now coming to the third one, the question of the reduction of the human consciousness of self and the creativeness of the human mind.

[24] See *Objective Knowledge*, Chapter 8; and *The Self and Its Brain*, esp. Chapter P3, section 19.

As Sir John Eccles has often stressed, this third question is the problem of the 'mind-brain liaison'; and Jacques Monod calls the problem of the human central nervous system the 'second frontier', comparing its difficulty with the 'first frontier', the problem of the origin of life.

No doubt this second frontier is a dangerous region to dwell in, especially for a lay biologist; nevertheless I may say that the attempts at a partial reduction seem to me more hopeful in this region than in that of the second question. As in the region of the first question, it seems to me that more new problems can be discovered here with reductionist methods, and perhaps even solved, than in the region of the second question—a region which looks to me comparatively sterile. I hardly need to stress that a completely successful reduction in any of the three regions seems to me most unlikely, if not impossible.

With this, it may perhaps be said, I have fulfilled my promise to discuss, or at any rate mention, these three outstanding questions of reduction listed at the beginning of this essay. But I wish to say a little more about the third of them—about the body-mind problem, or mind-body problem—before proceeding to my thesis of the incompletability of all science.

I regard the problem of the emergence of consciousness in animals (question 2), of understanding it and perhaps of reducing it to physiology, as most likely insoluble; and I feel similarly about the further problem of the emergence of the specifically human consciousness of self (question 3)—that is, the body-mind problem. But I do think that we can throw at least some light upon the problem of the human self.

I am in many ways a Cartesian dualist[25] even though I prefer to describe myself as a pluralist; and of course I do not subscribe to either of Descartes's two substances. Matter, we have seen, is no ultimate substance with the essential property of extension, but consists of complex structures about whose constitution we

[25] See *Conjectures and Refutations*, Chapter 12; and *The Self and Its Brain*, especially Chapter P4.

152

know a great deal, including an explanation of most of its 'extension': it takes up much space (if not all) through electrical repulsion.

My first thesis is that the human consciousness of self, with its apparently irreducible unity, is highly complex, and that it may perhaps be, in part, explicable.

I have suggested[26] that the higher human consciousness, or consciousness of selfhood, is absent in animals. I have also suggested that Descartes's conjecture that locates the human soul in the pineal gland may not be as absurd as it has often been represented to be, and that, in view of Sperry's results with divided brain hemispheres,[27] the location may have to be looked for in the speech centre, in the left hemisphere of the brain. As Eccles has more recently informed me,[28] Sperry's later experiments support this guess to a degree: the right brain may be described as that of a very clever animal while only the left brain appears to be human, and aware of selfhood.

I had based my guess upon the role which I ascribe to the development of a specifically human language.

All animal language—indeed, almost all animal behaviour—has an *expressive* (or symptomatic) and a *communicative* (or signalling) function, as Karl Bühler has pointed out.[29] But human language has, besides, some further functions, which are characteristic of it and make it a 'language' in a narrower and more important sense of the word. Bühler drew attention to the basic *descriptive* function of human language, and I pointed out later[30] that there are further functions (such as prescriptive, advisory and so on), of which the most important and characteristic one for human beings is the *argumentative* function. (Alf Ross points out

[26] In a course of lectures given at Emory University in May 1969, and over many years in my lectures at the London School of Economics. See also *The Self and Its Brain*, pp. 126, 438–48, 519.

[27] See *The Self and Its Brain*, especially Chapters E4 and E5.

[28] J. C. Eccles: 'Unconscious actions emanating from the human cerebral cortex', unpublished, 1972.

[29] Karl Bühler: *Sprachtheorie*, 1934.

[30] See *Conjectures and Refutations*, Chapters 4 and 12.

that many other functions may be added: for example, those of giving orders or making requests or promises.[31])

I have never thought that any of these functions are reducible to any of the others, least of all the two higher functions (description and argument) to the two lower ones (expression and communication). These, incidentally, are always present, which may perhaps be the reason why so many philosophers mistake them for those properties that are characteristic of human language.

My thesis is that, with the higher functions of the human language, a new world emerges: the world of the products of the human mind. I have called it 'World 3'. I have already described how I use this term—and also 'World 1' and 'World 2'—in the Afterword to this volume. Briefly, I call the world of physical matter, fields of force, and so on, 'World 1'; the world of consciousness and perhaps also subconscious experience 'World 2'; and 'World 3' especially the world of spoken (written or printed) language, like story telling, myth making, theories, theoretical problems, detecting mistakes, and arguments. (The worlds of artistic products and of social institutions may either be subsumed under World 3 or be called 'World 4' and 'World 5': this is just a matter of taste and convenience.)

I introduced these terms in order to emphasize the (limited) *autonomy* of these regions. Most materialists or physicalists or reductionists assert that, of these three worlds, only World 1 really exists, and that it is therefore autonomous. They replace World 2 by behaviour, and World 3, more particularly, by verbal behaviour. (As indicated above, this is just one of those all too easy ways of solving the body-mind problem: the way of denying the existence of the human mind and of a human consciousness of self—that is, of those things which I regard as some of the most remarkable and astonishing in the universe; the other equally easy way out is Berkeley's and Mach's immaterialism: the thesis that only sensations exist, and that matter is just a 'construct' out of sensations.)

[31] Alf Ross: 'The rise and fall of the doctrine of performatives' in *Contemporary Philosophy in Scandinavia*, ed. R. E. Olsen and A.M. Paul, 1972, pp. 197–212.

XIV

There are in the main four positions with respect to the inter-relationship between the body, or the brain, and the mind.

(1) A denial of the existence of the World 1 of physical states; that is, immaterialism, as held by Berkeley and Mach.

(2) A denial of the existence of the World 2 of mental states or events, a view common to certain materialists, physicalists and philosophical behaviourists, or philosophers upholding the identity of brain and mind.

(3) An assertion of a thoroughgoing parallelism between mental states and states of the brain; a position that is called 'psychophysical parallelism'. This was first introduced in the Cartesian school by Geulincx, Spinoza, Malebranche and Leibniz, mainly in order to avoid certain difficulties in the Cartesian view. (Like epiphenomenalism, it robs consciousness of any biological function.)

(4) An assertion that mental states can interact with physical states. This was the view of Descartes which, it is widely believed, was superseded by (3).

My own position is that a brain-mind parallelism is almost bound to exist *up to a point*. Certain reflexes, such as blinking when seeing a suddenly approaching object, are to all appearances of a more or less parallelistic character: the muscular reaction (in which no doubt the central nervous system is involved) repeats itself with regularity when the visual impression is repeated. If our attention is drawn to it we may be conscious of its happening, and so with some (but of course not all) other reflexes.

Nevertheless, I believe that the thesis of a *complete* psychophysical parallelism—position (3)—is a mistake, probably even in some cases where mere reflexes are involved. *I thus propose a form of psychophysical interactionism.* This involves (as was seen by Descartes) *the thesis that the physical World 1 is not causally closed,* but open to World 2, open to mental states and events. This is perhaps a somewhat unattractive thesis for the physicist, but it is I think one that is supported by the fact that World 3 (including its autonomous regions) acts upon World 1

155

through World 2. (Much of this has been discussed in the Afterword to this volume.)

I am willing to accept the view that whenever anything goes on in World 2, something connected with it goes on in World 1 (in the brain). But to speak of a complete or thoroughgoing parallelism, we would have to be able to assert that 'the same' mental state or event is always accompanied by an exactly corresponding physiological state, and *vice versa*.

As indicated, I am prepared to admit that there is something correct in this assertion, and that for example the electrical stimulation of certain brain regions may regularly give rise to certain characteristic movements or sensations. But I ask whether, as a universal rule about all mental states, the assertion has any content—whether it is not an empty assertion? For we can have a parallelism between World 2 elements and brain processes, or between World 2 *Gestalten* and brain processes, but we can hardly speak of a parallelism between a highly complex, unique and unanalysable World 2 process and some brain process. And there are many World 2 events in our lives which are unique. Even if we disregard creative novelty, hearing a melody twice and recognizing that it is the same melody is not a repetition of the same World 2 event, just because the second hearing of the melody is connected with an act of *recognizing* the melody, which was absent the first time. The World 1 object (in this case also a World 3 object) is repeated, not the World 2 event. Only if we could accept a kind of World 2 theory which, like associationist psychology, looks upon World 2 events as composed of recurring elements could we make a clear distinction between the repeated part of the World 2 experience—the *hearing* of the same melody—and the non-repeated part, the *recognition* that it is the same melody (where the recognition experience in its turn is capable of recurrence in other contexts). But I think that it is clear that such an atomistic or analytical psychology is quite incapable of carrying us far.

World 2 is highly complex. If we attend only to such fields as sense perception (that is, perception of World 1 objects) we may think that we can analyse World 2 by atomic or molecular methods, for instance *Gestalt* methods (methods which, I think, are all unrewarding as compared with the biological or functional methods of Egon Brunswik). But the application of such methods turns out to be quite inadequate if we consider our unique attempts to invent, and to understand, a World 3 object, such as a problem or a theory.

The way in which our thinking or our understanding interacts with attempts at linguistic formulation and is influenced by it; the way in which we have first a vague feeling for a problem or a theory which becomes clearer when we try to formulate it, and still clearer when we write it down and criticize our attempts to solve it; the way in which a problem may change and still be in a sense the old problem; the way in which a train of thought is on the one hand interconnected and on the other hand, articulated: all this seems to me to be beyond analytical or atomistic methods, including the interesting molecular methods of *Gestalt* psychology. (Incidentally, while Gestalt psychologists teach that hypotheses are Gestalten, I teach that Gestalten are hypotheses: interpretations of signals received.)

Besides, we have reason to believe that often, if one region of the brain is destroyed, another region can 'take over', with very little or perhaps no interference with World 2—another argument against parallelism, and this time based on experiments in World 1 rather than on the necessarily vague consideration of the more complex World 2 experiences.

All this sounds, of course, very anti-reductionist; and as a philosopher who looks at this world of ours, with us in it, I indeed despair of any ultimate reduction. But methodologically this does not lead me to an anti-reductionist research programme. It only leads to the prediction that with the growth of our attempted reductions, our knowledge will expand; and, with it, the range of our unsolved problems.

XV

Let us now return to the problem of the specifically human consciousness of self; my suggestion was that it emerges through

157

the interaction (feedback, if you like) between World 2 and the Worlds 1 and 3. My arguments for the role played by World 3 are as follows.

The human consciousness of self is based, among other things, upon a number of highly abstract *theories*. Animals and even plants have, no doubt, a sense of time, and temporal expectations. But it needs an almost explicit *theory* of time (*pace* Benjamin Lee Whorf) to look upon oneself as possessing a past, a present and a future; as having a personal history; and as being aware of one's personal identity (linked to the identity of one's body) throughout this history. Thus it is a *theory* that, during the period of sleep, when we lose the continuity of consciousness, we—our bodies—remain essentially the same; and it is on the basis of this theory that we can consciously recall past events (instead of merely being influenced by them in our expectations and reactions which, I suggest, is the more primitive form which the memory of animals takes).

Some animals no doubt have personalities; they have something closely analogous to pride and ambition, and they learn to respond to a name. But the human consciousness of self is anchored in language and (both explicitly and implicitly) in formulated theories. A child learns to use his name of himself, and ultimately a word like 'ego' or 'I', and he learns to use it with the consciousness of the continuity of his body, and of himself; he also combines it with the knowledge that consciousness is not always unbroken. The great complexity and the nonsubstantial character of the human soul, or the human self, become particularly clear if we remember that there are cases where men have forgotten who they are; they have forgotten part or the whole of their past history, but they have retained, or perhaps recovered, at least part of their selfhood. In a sense, their memory has not been lost, for they *remember how* to walk, to eat, and even to speak. But they do not *remember that* they come from, say, Bristol, or what their names and addresses are. In so far as they do not find their way home (which animals normally do) their consciousness of self is affected even beyond the normal level of

158

animal memory. But if they have not lost the power of speech, some human consciousness is left that goes beyond animal memory.

I am not a great friend of psychoanalysis, but its findings seem to support the view of the complexity of the human self, in contrast to any Cartesian appeal to a thinking substance. My main point is that the consciousness of the human self involves, at the very least, an awareness of the (highly theoretical) temporal or historical continuity of one's body; an awareness of the connection between one's conscious memory and the single, unique body which is one's own; and the consciousness of the normal and periodical interruption of one's consciousness by sleep (which, again, involves a theory of time and temporal periodicity). Moreover, it involves the consciousness of belonging locally and socially to a certain place and circle of people. No doubt much of this has an instinctive basis and is shared by animals. My thesis is that in raising it even to the level of unspoken human consciousness, human language or interaction between Worlds 2 and 3 plays an important role.

Clearly, the unity of the human self is largely due to memory, and memory can be ascribed not only to animals but also to plants (and even perhaps, in some sense, to non-organic structures such as magnets). It is therefore most important to see that the appeal to memory as such is not enough to explain the unity of the human self. What is needed is not so much the 'ordinary' memory (of past events), but a memory of theories that link the consciousness of having a body to World 3 theories about bodies (that is, to physics); a memory which is of the character of a 'grasp' of World 3 theories. It comprises the dispositions which enable us to fall back on explicit World 3 theories if we need to, with the feeling that we possess such dispositions and that we can make use of them in order to articulate those theories if we need to. (This would, of course, explain to a certain extent the difference between the human consciousness of self with its dependence on human language, and animal consciousness.)

159

XVI

These facts seem to me to establish the impossibility of any reduction of the human World 2, the world of human consciousness, to the human World 1, that is, essentially, to brain physiology. For World 3 is, at least in part, autonomous and independent of the other two worlds. If the autonomous part of World 3 can interact with World 2, then World 2, or so it seems to me, cannot be reducible to World 1.

My standard examples of the partial autonomy of World 3 are taken from arithmetic.

As already explained in the Afterword to this volume, the infinite series of natural numbers provides such an example. It is an invention, a product, of the human mind, and a part of developed human language. There are, it appears, primitive languages in which one can count only 'one, two, many' and others in which one can count only to five. But once a method of counting without end has been invented, distinctions and problems arise autonomously: even and odd numbers are not *invented* but *discovered* in the series of natural numbers, and so are prime numbers, and the many solved and unsolved problems connected with them.

These problems, and the theorems which solve them (such as Euclid's theorem that there does not exist a greatest prime) arise autonomously; they arise as part of the internal structure of the man-created series of natural numbers, and independently of what we think or fail to think. But we can *grasp* or *understand* or *discover* these problems, and solve some of them. Thus our thinking, which belongs to World 2, depends in part on the autonomous problems and on the objective truth of theorems which belong to World 3: World 2 not only creates World 3, it is partly created by World 3 in a kind of feedback process.

My argument then runs as follows: World 3, and especially its autonomous part, are clearly irreducible to the physical World 1. But since World 2 depends, in part, upon World 3, it is also irreducible to World 1.

Physicalists, or philosophical reductionists as I have called

160

them, are thus reduced to denying the existence of Worlds 2 and 3. But with this, the whole of human technology (especially the existence of computers), which makes so much use of World 3 theorems, becomes incomprehensible; and we must assume that such violent changes in World 1 as are produced by the builders of airports or skyscrapers are ultimately produced, without the invention of World 3 theories or World 2 plans based on them, by the physical World 1 itself: they are predestined; they are part of a pre-established harmony built, ultimately, into hydrogen nuclei.

These results seem to me absurd; and philosophical behaviourism or physicalism (or the philosophy of the identity of mind and body) appears to me to be reduced to this absurdity.

XVII

Philosophical reductionism is, I believe, a mistake. It is due to the wish to reduce everything to an ultimate explanation in terms of essences and substances, that is, to an explanation which is neither capable of, nor in need of, any further explanation.

Once we give up the theory of ultimate explanation we realize that we can always continue to ask 'Why?'. Why-questions never lead to an ultimate answer. Intelligent children seem to know this, but give way to the adults who, indeed, cannot possibly have time enough to answer what is in principle an endless series of questions.

XVIII

The Worlds 1, 2, and 3, though partly autonomous, belong to the same universe: they interact. But it can easily be shown that knowledge of the universe, if this knowledge itself forms part of the universe, as it does, must be incompletable.

In the Afterword, I have mentioned the example of the man who draws a detailed map of the room in which he is working, and the problems that arise when he begins to include in his drawing the map which he is drawing. It is clear that he cannot complete the task.

This example and others help show why all explanatory science is incompletable; for to be complete it would have to give an explanatory account of itself.

An even stronger result is implicit in Gödel's famous theorem of the incompletability of formalized arithmetic (though to use Gödel's theorem and other metamathematical incompleteness theorems in this context is to use heavy armament against a comparatively weak position). Since all physical science uses arithmetic (and since for a reductionist only science formulated in physical symbols has any reality), Gödel's incompleteness theorem renders all physical science incomplete; which to the reductionist should show that all science is incomplete. For the nonreductionist, who does not believe in the reducibility of all science to physically formulated science, science is incomplete anyway.

Not only is philosophical reductionism a mistake, but the belief that the method of reduction can achieve complete reductions is, it seems, mistaken too. We live in a world of emergent evolution; of problems whose solutions, if they are solved, beget new and deeper problems. Thus we live in a universe of emergent novelty; of a novelty which, as a rule, is not completely reducible to any of the preceding stages.

Nevertheless, the method of attempting reductions is most fruitful, not only because we learn a great deal by its partial successes, by partial reductions, but also because we learn from our partial failures, from the new problems which our failures reveal. Open problems are almost as interesting as their solutions; indeed they would be just as interesting but for the fact that almost every solution opens up in its turn a whole new world of open problems.

FURTHER REMARKS ON REDUCTION, 1981

I

When writing the foregoing Addendum early in 1972, I was intent on bringing out two things. One is the value of the attempt to reduce: the often quite incredible success of such attempts, and the new understanding which they may produce. The other was that we nonetheless have no really completely successful reductions, where 'successful' means more than just adding to our insight, to our understanding: where it means that one province of knowledge, such as chemistry, has been shown to be completely derivable from another province of knowledge, such as atomic theory.

In raising a strong doubt whether such complete reductions exist, I wanted to combat what I called 'philosophical reductionism', the somewhat dogmatic anticipation that reductions will, sooner or later, completely succeed, for some philosophical reason; in other words, that they will succeed because we know enough about the world, or about ourselves, or about language, or about science, or about philosophy, or about I do not know what, to know that reductionism is true.

To those who say so I reply that we know nothing of the kind, and that the world is far more interesting and exciting than is dreamt of in the reductionist philosophy.

II

I still vividly remember the excitement of the discovery of the element 72 (Hafnium) in 1922, as a result of Niels Bohr's marvellous quantum theory of the periodic system of elements. It

163

struck us then as the great moment when chemistry had been reduced to atomic theory; and it was, I am still inclined to say, the greatest moment in all the reductionist adventures of the twentieth century, superseded perhaps only by the breakthrough represented by Crick and Watson's discovery of the structure of DNA. I still possess a textbook from the year 1929 in which the progress is dramatically depicted by two diagrams which I reproduce here (in grateful memory of their author, Arthur Haas, and of my friend Franz Urbach, who assisted him in its completion).[1]

Bohr's theory led not only to the prediction of the chemical properties of the elements, and thereby to the prediction of the properties of the still unknown element 72 and thus to its discovery, but it also allowed the prediction of some of their optical properties; and it even led to the prediction of some of the properties of the chemical compounds.

It was a great moment in the history of matter. We felt, rightly, *this was it*: Bohr had hit rock bottom. And yet, a quite different

	I a	I b	II a	II b	III a	III b	IV a	IV b	V a	V b	VI a	VI b	VII a	VII b	VIII a	VIII b
1	1 H															2 He
2	3 Li		4 Be		5 B		6 C		7 N		8 O		9 F			10 Ne
3	11 Na		12 Mg		13 Al		14 Si		15 P		16 S		17 Cl			18 Ar
4	19 K	29 Cu	20 Ca	30 Zn	21 Sc	31 Ga	22 Ti	32 Ge	23 V	33 As	24 Cr	34 Se	25 Mn	35 Br	26 Fe 27 Co 28 Ni	36 Kr
5	37 Rb	47 Ag	38 Sr	48 Cd	39 Y	49 In	40 Zr	50 Sn	41 Nb	51 Sb	42 Mo	52 Te	43 Ma	53 J	44 Ru 45 Rh 46 Pd	54 X
6	55 Cs	79 Au	56 Ba	80 Hg	57—71 seltene Erden	81 Tl	72 Hf	82 Pb	73 Ta	83 Bi	74 W	84 Po	75 Re	85	76 Os 77 Ir 78 Pt	86 Em
7	87		88 Ra		89 Ac		90 Th		91 Pa		92 U					

Table 1.
The Periodic System of the Chemical Elements,
ordered according to atomic weight
and to chemical and other phenomena.

[1] Arthur Haas: *Atomtheorie* (Berlin and Leipzig, 1929), pp. 35 and 111. [See Popper's discussion of Urbach in *Unended Quest*, pp. 84, 91, 128. Ed.]

164

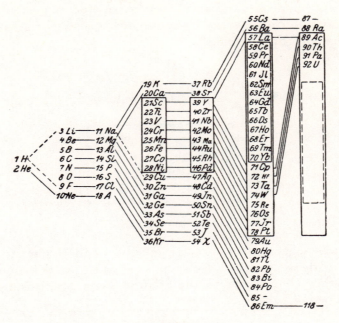

Table 2.
The Periodic System according to Niels Bohr's Theory
of the Shell Structure of Atoms

type of problem already was looming in the background, started by a suggestion of Soddy's (1910) and a discovery of J. J. Thomson's (1913, the year of Bohr's atom model), and by F. W. Aston's mass spectroscopy (1919). And then came Urey's bombshell, the discovery of heavy water, which meant that all the basic measurements of chemistry, the measurements of the atomic weights—the basic phenomena of chemistry and of the periodic system—were slightly wrong, and had to be revised.

Thus the rock bottom suddenly gave way: somehow Niels Bohr had built on a morass. But his edifice still stood.

Then came quantum mechanics, and the theory of London and Heitler. And it became fairly clear that the reduction of chemistry to physics was a reduction in principle only; and that anything like a complete reduction was now further distant than it had seemed in 1922, the year of the great breakthrough.

This is a glimpse of the story, sketched in order to make things less abstract, for I now come to a somewhat abstract chapter: to the logic of reductionism.

III

Peter Medawar critically discusses reduction,[2] using the following Table 3:

```
(4) Ecology/Sociology
(3) Biology
(2) Chemistry
(1) Physics
```

Table 3.
Customary Table of Reduction

Medawar suggests that the true relation of the higher to the lower of these subjects is not simply one of logical reducibility, but rather comparable to the relation between the subjects mentioned in Table 4.

```
(4) Metrical (Euclidean) Geometry
(3) Affine Geometry
(2) Projective Geometry
(1) Topology
```

Table 4.
Various Geometries

The fundamental relation between the higher geometrical disciplines listed in Table 4 and the lower ones is not quite easy to describe, but it is certainly not one of reducibility. For example, metrical geometry, especially in the form of Euclidean geometry, is only very partially reducible to projective geometry, even though the results of projective geometry are all valid in a metrical geometry embedded in a language rich enough to employ the

---

[2] See *The Self and Its Brain*, pp. 20–21; and also P. B. Medawar, *Induction and Intuition in Scientific Thought*, London, 1969, pp. 15–19, and 'A Geometric Model of Reduction and Emergence', in Ayala and Dobzhansky, *op. cit.*, pp. 57–63.

concepts of projective geometry. Thus we may regard metrical geometry as an *enrichment* of projective geometry. Similar relations hold between the other levels of Table 4. The enrichment is partly one of concepts, but mainly one of theorems.

Medawar proposes that the relations between consecutive levels of Table 3 may be analogous to those of Table 4. Thus chemistry may be regarded as an enrichment of physics; which explains why it is partly though not wholly reducible to physics; and similarly the higher levels of Table 3.

Thus the subjects in Table 4 are clearly *not reducible* to the ones on lower levels, even though the lower levels remain, in a very clear sense, valid within the higher levels, and even though they are somehow contained in the higher levels. Moreover, *some* of the propositions on the higher levels are reducible to the lower levels.

I find Medawar's remarks highly suggestive. They are, of course, acceptable only if we give up the idea that our physical universe is deterministic—that physical theory, together with the initial conditions prevalent at some given moment, *completely* determine the state of the physical universe at any other moment. Were we to accept this Laplacean determinism, Table 3 could not be regarded as analogous to Table 4.

As it is, the higher levels of both these tables can be regarded as containing new fundamental hypotheses (new axioms), not derivable from the hypotheses (axioms) of the lower levels, and new fundamental concepts, not definable in terms of the concepts of the lower levels.

As opposed to this, the idea of reductionism is that nothing intrinsically new enters at the higher levels.

Thus, if we formalize (axiomatize) our physical hypotheses, then, according to reductionism, every apparently new concept should be reducible (definable) in terms of the concepts of physics, and therefore in principle avoidable; and every apparently new hypothesis should, in the presence of these definitions, be logically deducible from the basic hypotheses of the formalized or axiomatized system of physics.

IV

Now there are logical reasons to doubt whether this reductionist programme, which can be described in purely logical terms, can be carried out even in principle. I shall mention a few of these reasons.

Consider a similar programme, the programme of reducing mathematics to logic: the programme that culminated in Whitehead and Russell's *Principia Mathematica,* a splendid achievement, but, in the judgement of the most competent mathematicians, also a failure, at least as far as the reductionist aspects of the programme are concerned. Pure logic does play an immensely important part in mathematics. But mathematics is richer than (functional) logic. This can be seen from Gödel's discoveries: in every axiom system for number theory there arise problems which cannot be logically decided in that axiom system but only in a stronger one. (In this stronger system, new but exactly analogous problems arise.) Thus we need an infinite sequence of growing axiom systems, and even the reduction of one of these (incomplete) axiom systems for number theory to logic would not be a complete reduction in the sense of the reductionist programme.

There is also the problem of definitions. The point of a formal definition in the sense of the reductionist programme is that it serves as a *mere abbreviation.* W. V. Quine, for example, after introducing some definitions into his system of mathematical logic, comments upon them as follows:

> Such conventions of abbreviation are called formal definitions. . . .
> To define a sign formally is to adopt it as a shorthand for some form of notation already at hand. . . . To define a sign is to show how to avoid it.[3]

This is the kind of definition which the reductionist has in mind; for he wishes to show that no intrinsically new, no

---

[3] W. V. Quine, *Mathematical Logic,* revised edition, 1951, p. 47.

irreducible element enters on the higher levels: *everything* is reducible to the lowest level, physics; although, owing to complicated physical situations or constellations, abbreviating definitions become necessary (for reasons of what Mach called 'economy of thought').

Let us call such purely abbreviating definitions 'non-creative definitions'. For there are also other definitions, creative definitions. They are formally indistinguishable from the non-creative ones, but they play an entirely different role—the role of axioms, or of new hypotheses; and their use is, therefore, impermissible in an attempted reduction.

V

Creative and non-creative definitions can be described as follows.

Let S be the new symbol which a certain formal definition introduces. If the definition is non-creative, or merely abbreviative, then all the *new theorems*—that is, those theorems whose derivation the definition allows, and which cannot be derived without the definition—will contain the symbol S; and the definition will allow us to eliminate the symbol S from every one of these new theorems. If, however, the definition is 'creative', then there will be theorems which do not contain the symbol S but which are not derivable from the axioms in the absence of that definition which introduces S.

First impressions may suggest that such creative definitions cannot exist. However, they can and do exist; and some of the facts about them bear heavily upon the reductionist programme.

In 1963 I published a case study, "Creative and Non Creative Definitions in the Calculus of Probability".[4] I took the calculus of probability as the object of my case study for various reasons, mainly because it presented me with an axiom system I thought I knew fairly well, and because I was fairly familiar with the methods of proving whether an axiom (or a definition) was able to

[4] *Synthese* **15**, 1963, pp. 167–186.

yield new theorems, that is, theorems not derivable from the rest of the axiom system.

The main results of the case study which interest us here are the following two (for which examples are given in that study):

If we introduce a purely abbreviative or non-creative definition in an axiom system, then *this definition can become a creative definition*:

(a) by omitting one of the axioms
(b) by adding a new axiom.

We can thus never be sure of a definition's being creative or non-creative unless our axiom system is strictly fixed.

Now this is of course most important from the point of view of 'physicalism', that is, from the thesis that (at least) the whole of chemistry and biology can be reduced to physics: we cannot say of any apparently purely abbreviative definition whether it is really abbreviative unless the axiom system of physics with which we work (to which we wish to reduce the higher systems) is precisely formalized and fixed.

But even then the character of some definition may remain in doubt. There is no routine method of deciding whether a given definition is, relative to a given axiom system, creative or not.

It seems to me that this shows that, from a purely logical point of view, the programme of reductionism is very vague indeed. Of course, from the point of view of understanding a science intuitively—a very important though vague aspect—even partial reductions may remain desirable and important.

VI

All this bears upon the history of materialism, and upon the story of the self-transcendence of materialism.

The main idea behind materialism, the materialist research programme, as I call it,[5] was the attempt to explain all things—the

---

[5] See the 'Metaphysical Epilogue' to *Quantum Theory and the Schism in Physics*, Volume III of the *Postscript to the Logic of Scientific Discovery*.

All, the ordered universe, the Cosmos—in terms of the known, and familiar, properties of matter.

There were, in the main, two materialistic research programmes. One, going back to Parmenides, regarded the world as full, as filled with matter; it led to continuum mechanics. The other, taking 'atoms and the void' as its slogan, regarded the world as largely empty. Both programmes led to a view of the world as a huge mechanical machine: either of vortices; or of atoms. But it was essential to both programmes that the world be explained in terms of familiar properties of matter.

This essential demand is of course a reductionist one. In this regard, materialism and reductionism are one and the same programme. It was a most important and fruitful programme— one that indeed became the science of nature. Yet it transcended itself; thanks to the critical tradition of science, which proved stronger than the ideological tradition.

Thus, in the place of those familiar properties which should have done the explaining, as anticipated in the original programme, we now have abstract and unfamiliar laws; and the familiar behaviour of matter is explained by very unfamiliar abstract mathematical formulae. For example, the intuitively highly satisfying idea of the conservation of matter has been replaced by the highly abstract law of the conservation of energy; and matter itself is regarded as only a form of this abstract energy.

But this process of transcending materialism started earlier— with Newton and Newtonian forces, with Faraday and Maxwell and Einstein, and the idea of fields. And with ideas such as an intrinsic probability of atomic disintegration (half-life).[6]

VII

None of these reductionist efforts explain the creativity of the universe: life, and its incredible intricacies and wealth of forms. In fact, before Darwin a reductionist could do no more than shut his eyes to the problem of design in nature. After the publication,

[6] See *The Self and Its Brain*, especially Chapters P1, P3, and P5.

in 1859, of *The Origin of Species,* there was an argument—natural selection—a very strong argument indeed, which could be used by reductionism. Reductionists no longer had to shut their eyes in order not to see the problem of design; quite the contrary, they could now use the problem of design on behalf of reductionism.

The Darwinian reduction programme received its greatest encouragement through the success of Watson and Crick. No wonder that molecular biology became not only an extremely fast growing part of science but, at the same time, almost an ideology.

VIII

Here I wish to say a few words about another exciting recent development that bears importantly on the question of the evolution of life: the development of the thermodynamics of open systems far from equilibrium.

'Thermodynamics' is another word for the flow of heat, and the forces that are responsible for it. Heat flows, as everybody knows, from the hotter body or region to the colder one, and this movement tends to equilibrium, when the flow stops. Thermodynamics as a science tries to describe all this; and a successful reductionist and materialist explanation is given by the corresponding molecular mechanics, called statistical mechanics.

The first two laws of thermodynamics are the law of conservation of energy and the law that asserts that entropy can only increase. Expressed in terms of the Boltzmannian interpretation of entropy as molecular disorder, the second law says that the molecular disorder of a closed system can only increase until it reaches its maximum—total disorder.

This law of the increase of disorder, interpreted as a cosmic principle, made the evolution of life incomprehensible, apparently even paradoxical. For the evolution of life shows a general tendency away from Boltzmannian disorder.

It has been suspected for a long time that the solution of this apparent paradox is connected with the fact that every living system, and even the whole earth, with its developing and growing flora and fauna, is *an open system.*

172

Of course the second law (and Boltzmann's interpretation of it) does not hold for open systems; so there seemed to be a possibility here of making some progress.

Spectacular progress now has been made. I cannot tell the story here, but I wish to mention the most important results, due mainly to Prigogine.[7] They are, in brief, that *open systems in a state far from equilibrium* show no tendency towards increasing disorder, even though they produce entropy. But they can export this entropy into their environment, and can increase rather than decrease their internal order. They can develop structural properties, and thereby do the very opposite of turning into an equilibrium state in which nothing exciting can happen to them any longer.

Perhaps the simplest example is a tea kettle at the boil on a hotplate. This is an open system in the sense that a lot of energy flows into it from the bottom and out of it at the top and at the sides.

Inside the system, strong temperature differences develop, the very opposite of what a closed system would do. They produce not only flow of heat but fast water currents, and when the water starts boiling we even have the production of visible material structures of fairly characteristic size: steam bubbles. These steam bubbles are far from equal, but there is a kind of average size: a typical probabilistic or statistical effect (such propensities depend on the total situation: temperature of the hotplate, size and shape of the kettle, heat flow . . .). Moreover, there is a division of the water into two states—liquid water and steam; and it is, clearly, a probabilistic problem whether a group of molecules will assume one state or the other during the next unit of time: we are faced here (as throughout in thermodynamics) with probabilistic effects, with a non-deterministic part of physics.

Prigogine is developing this part of physics, both theoretically and experimentally, and it is now clear that open systems in a state

[7] Ilya Prigogine: *From Being to Becoming: Time and Complexity in the Physical Sciences* (San Francisco, 1980), esp. pp. 88–9.

far from equilibrium can build up new structures rather than move towards a state of equilibrium, of maximization of entropy, of the disappearance of structure: of that heat death that has so long been predicted for the universe.

IX

Prigogine's work may be looked upon as a piece of exciting physicalist reduction, at least in the sense that it takes the first steps towards a physical understanding of the evolution of higher structures (which seems to be a fairly obvious aspect of the evolution of life on earth). It may thus open the way to understanding the reason why the creativeness of life does not *contradict* the laws of physics.

But although this is a step in the reductionist direction, it is infinitely far from a reduction of the creative properties of life.

Whether or not we look at the universe as a physical machine, we should face the fact that it has produced life and creative men; that it is open to their creative thoughts, and has been physically changed by them. We must not close our eyes to this fact or permit our appreciation of the successes wrought by reductionist programmes to blind us to the fact that the universe that harbours life is creative in the best sense: creative in the sense in which the great poets, the great artists, the great musicians have been creative, as well as the great mathematicians, the great scientists, and the great inventors.

INDICES

compiled by Stephen Kresge and Nancy Artis Sadoyama

References in italics indicate passages of special importance. A page number followed by '*t*' indicates that the term is discussed in the place referred to; '*n*' means 'footnote', and '*q*' (in the Index of Names) means 'quoted'. The reader is also advised to consult the Indices to the other volumes of the *Postscript*.

Index of Names

Index of Subjects

jective versus subjective, 96; testing of, 97–99

Probability statements, and general hypothesis of randomness, 102; and Landé's blade, 100, 102–104; of single events, *section* 29

Probability theory, a physical theory of, 93

Problem, objective, 119–122

Problem solving, and consciousness, 150

Propensities, *section* 27; compared to forces, 95; fluctuating forces and, 94; incompatible with determinism, 93; and Landé's blade, *section* 30; and objective situation, 94; as physical possibilities, 105; a physical theory of, *section* 27; and statistical conclusions, 106

Pseudo-argument, 4

Psychology, arguments for determinism from, *section* 7; and Hume's idea of 'inference from motives', 20; Kant's acceptance of, 20, 23; and the principle of accountability, 23–25

Psychophysical interactionism, 155–157. *See also* Worlds 1, 2, and 3

Psychophysical parallelism, 155

QUANTUM JUMPS, 125&*n*

Quantum theory, 2, 125–126, 139–146, 163–165; and determinism, 5, 124–126, *section* 10; as electromagnetic theory of matter, 139; and human freedom, 126; a probabilistic theory, 29; and reduction of chemistry to quantum physics, 142–143, 147, 165

RANDOMNESS, the general hypothesis of, 102

Rationality, 84–85, 87–88, 126

Realism, 2*n*–3*n*

Reality, and World 1, 116

Reduction, reductionism, attempted, of electricity and magnetism to Newtonian mechanics, 124, 135–136; of biology to chemistry and physics, 131, 148–150, 170; Cartesian, 135; of chemistry to physics, 132, 140–147,

149, 164, 165; of consciousness to biology or to chemistry and physics, 131, 151, 157–159; contrasted with explanation, 132–133&*n*, 134–135; Darwinian, 172; Einsteinian, 137–138; and four functions of language, 153–154; logic of, 166–170; of mathematics to logic, 168–169; Maxwellian, 138; of mechanics and chemistry to electromagnetic theory of matter, 139–140; Medawar's criticism of, 166–167; as method, 132; Newtonian, 136–137; philosophical, 132&*n*–133*n*, 146, 161–162, 163; Prigogine and, 174; programmes of, in physics, 134–138; Pythagorean, 133; of rational fractions to ordered pairs of natural numbers, 133–134; questions of, 131–174; as successful form of scientific endeavour, 132, 137, 163; of Worlds 2 and 3 to World 1, 160

Relativity, general theory of, and Gödel's argument, 58*n*

Relativity, special theory of, not *prima facie* deterministic, *section* 19; and Gödel's argument, 3*n*, 58*n*; no Laplacean demon in, 60–61. *See also* Einstein's theory of; Relativity, general theory of

Religious determinism, 5–7, *sections* 12 & 25

Research programmes, biological, 145*n*; materialist, 170–171; metaphysical, 146&*n*; Pythagorean, 133

Responsibility, human, xx, 113

SCHLICK'S VIEW OF DETERMINISM, 3–4&*n*

Science, aims of, 45–47; searchlight theory of, 45*n*

'Scientific' determinism, xx*t*, 1–2*t*, 5*t*, 11*t*, *section* 1; 13, 23, 24, 42, Chapter II; alleged scientific character, xx; appeal to success of science, 33; argument from, and approximate character of knowledge, 55; arises from criticism of clocks & clouds analogy, 9; Einstein's change of mind regarding, 2&*n*–3&*n*, 124, *section* 26; and four functions of language, 82–85;

181

and impossibility of self-prediction, 77–78; Kant's strong belief in, 7, 20, 26; Laplacean, xx–xxi, 123–127; logical arguments against, 42; metaphysical arguments against, 42; must ignore differences between higher & lower functions of language, 84; not entailed by Newtonian mechanics, 7; and predictability from within, *section* 11; and *prima facie* deterministic theories, 32, *section* 13; refutation of, *sections* 17 & 23; 106; refuted by argument of Haldane, Descartes, and St. Augustine, *section* 24; requires accountability, *sections* 3 & 7; and special relativity, 61; stronger version of, 13, 37, 38, refuted by Hadamard's result, *section* 14; two definitions of, *section* 12; third version, where description after event logically entails prediction, 79–80; third version and accountability, 79–80. *See also* Determinism; Indeterminism; Metaphysical determinism

Scientific theories, approximate character of, 55, 62; arguments from characteristics of theories to characteristics of world, 43–44, 45–46; fallibility of, 43; implications for Haldane's argument that world is repetitive, 46*n*; as more than instruments, 42; as nets to catch the world, *section* 15, 42, 47; as universal theories, 44–47

Self, human consciousness of, 151–154, 157–159

Self-prediction, impossibility of, *section* 22; and prediction task, 70–77; and proof that calculator cannot predict results of own calculations, 68–77. *See also* Knowledge, growth of; Predictability

Set theory, axiomatic, 134

Simplicity, as characteristic of scientific theory, 44–45

Stability, problem of, 31, *sections* 12 & 14; statistical, 98–99

'State', of Newtonian system, 29; question whether a system will ever be in a particular state, *section* 12

Statistical questions, and statistical theories, *sections* 28 & 29

TESTABILITY, and logical weakness, 8; of probabilistic theories, 97–99, *sections* 29 & 30; of propensities, 94; and preference of theories, 44

Theories, deterministic, *see Prima facie* deterministic theories

Theories, Scientific, *see there*

Thermodynamics, 172*t*

Time, arrow of, 55*n*–56*n*; interpreted as space coordinate, 3*n*; reality of, 3*n*

Truth, as aim of science, 42; Tarski on, 67*n*

UNIQUE ACHIEVEMENTS, alleged scientific predictability of, 41–42, 128

Uniqueness, of world, and approximate character of theories, 46

Universality, 45–46

Universe, creativity of, 171; essential openness of, 3*n*, 126, 128–130; theory of its origin, 143

WHY-QUESTIONS, *section* 2

Will, human, and Hobbes, 20&*n*

Worlds 1, 2, and 3 (three worlds, 114*t*–116; and emergence of human consciousness, 153–154, 157–161; interaction among, 117–118, 128, 155–162; and mind-body problem, 154–157; and psychological interactionism, 156–157

World 1 (physical world), 114, 127; alleged causal closedness towards Worlds 2 and 3, 124, 127, 155–157; confusing its character with that of World 3 theories about, 130; its openness, 127; its reality, 116–117

World 2 (experience or thought in the subjective sense), 114*t*; its causal openness to Worlds 1 and 3, 117–118; reality of, 117–118; 170–171

World 3 (objective thought, especially *products* of human mind), 114*t*–115*t*; autonomous properties of, 118–122, 130; its causal openness to Worlds 1 and 2, and its intrinsic openness, 116, 128–130; and Gödel's theorem, 128; and language, 118; and numbers, 120–121; reality of, 118–122

ABOUT THE AUTHOR

Sir KARL (RAIMUND) POPPER was born in Vienna in 1902. He studied mathematics, physics, psychology, education, the history of music, and philosophy at the University of Vienna from 1918 to 1928. At the same time he worked as a cabinet maker's apprentice and as a teacher. In 1978, fifty years after he took his Ph.D. degree, the University of Vienna 'renewed' this degree in a solemn ceremony and gave him an honorary doctorate in the natural sciences.

In 1934, when still a schoolteacher in Vienna, he published *Logik der Forschung,* a book that became a classic after its translation into English. (*The Logic of Scientific Discovery* was published in 1959.) It has now been translated into many languages and, after 54 years, it is still frequently reprinted.

Popper, who lives in England, has lectured in Europe, in New Zealand, Australia, India, Japan, and since 1950, when he delivered the William James Lectures in Philosophy at Harvard University, often in America. Among his books are *The Open Society and Its Enemies* (for which he received the Lippincott Award of the American Political Science Association); *Conjectures and Refutations; The Poverty of Historicism; Objective Knowledge; Unended Quest;* and three volumes constituting the *Postscript to the Logic of Scientific Discovery – Realism and the Aim of Science, The Open Universe: An Argument for Indeterminism*, and *Quantum Theory and the Schism in Physics.* Together with Sir John Eccles he published *The Self and Its Brain.*

183

He holds honorary degrees from the Universities of Chicago, Denver, Warwick, Canterbury (New Zealand), Salford, The City University (London), Vienna, Mannheim, Guelph (Canada), Frankfurt, Salzburg, Cambridge, Oxford, and Brasilia; and from Gustavus Adolphus College and the University of London.

He is a Fellow of the Royal Society (London), and of the British Academy; a Foreign Honorary Member, American Academy of Arts and Sciences; Membre de l'Institut de France; Socio Straniero dell' Accademia Nazionale dei Lincei; Membre de l'Académie Internationale de Philosophie des Sciences; Associate, Académie Royale de Belgique; Membre de l'Académie Européenne des Sciences, des Arts, et des Lettres; Hon. Member, the Royal Society of New Zealand; Membre d'Honneur, Académie Internationale d'Histoire des Sciences; Ehrenmitglied, Deutsche Akademie für Sprache und Dichtung; Ehrenmitglied, Österreichische Akademie der Wissenschaften; Ehrenmitglied, Gesellschaft der Ärtze, Wien; Foreign Associate, National Academy of Sciences, Washington D.C.

He is also an honorary member, Harvard Chapter of Phi Beta Kappa; Ehrenmitglied, Allgemeine Gesellschaft für Philosophie in Deutschland; Hon. Fellow, London School of Economics and Political Science; and Hon. Fellow, Darwin College, Cambridge; Honorary Research Fellow, Dept of History and Philosophy of Science, King's College, London; and Senior Research Fellow, Hoover Institution, Stanford University.

He was awarded the Prize of the City of Vienna for Moral and Mental Sciences; the Sonning Prize of the University of Copenhagen; the Dr Karl Renner Prize of the City of Vienna; the Dr Leopold Lucas Prize of the University of Tübingen; the Ehrenring of the City of Vienna; and the Prix Alexix de Tocqueville.

He received the Grand Decoration of Honour in Gold (Austria); the Gold Medal for Distinguished Service to Science of the American Museum of Natural History, New York; the Ehrenzeichen für Wissenschaft und Kunst (Austria); the Order Pour le Mérite (German Federal Republic); the Grand Cross of the Order of Merit with Star (German Fed. Rep.); and the Wissenschaftsmedaille der Stadt Linz.

In 1965 he was knighted by Queen Elizabeth II, who invested him in 1982 with the insignia of a Companion of Honour (H.C.).

ABOUT THE EDITOR

WILLIAM WARREN BARTLEY, III, a graduate of Harvard and the University of London, is a former student and colleague and a long-time associate of Sir Karl Popper. He has been Lecturer in Logic at the London School of Economics, Lecturer in the History of the Philosophy of Science at the Warburg Institute, and S. A. Cook Bye-Fellow at Gonville and Caius College, Cambridge. Formerly Professor of Philosophy and of the History and Philosophy of Science at the University of Pittsburgh, he is currently Senior Research Fellow at the Hoover Institution on War, Revolution and Peace at Stanford University.